which **plant** where

which plant where

ANTHONY ATHA, MARGARET CROWTHER & SUE HOOK

p

This is a Parragon Book
This edition published in 2006

Parragon
Queen Street House
4 Queen Street
Bath BA1 1HE, UK

Produced by The Bridgewater Book Company Ltd.

ISBN: 1-40546-381-3

Printed in China

NOTE
For growing and harvesting, calendar information applies
only to the Northern Hemisphere (US zones 5–9).

contents

introduction

Selecting and positioning plants in beds and borders can be a confusing part of gardening, while the wide range of plants now available from nurseries and garden centres is similarly bewildering. Knowing the most suitable plants for the style of garden you desire is an essential part of gardening – and this is where this all-colour book excels.

Which Plant Where is an inspirational yet practical book which guides gardeners through the selection of plants and where they are best used. It starts by exploring the basics of garden design and proceeds to give detailed information about gardening in climates and places that initially appear to be inhospitable. Coastal gardens, so often exposed to strong, buffeting wind laden with salt, are frequently considered to be difficult areas in which to garden, but once a hedge is planted and salt-spray resistant plants are established a garden soon flourishes.

Roof gardens are a continual delight but vulnerable to blustery winds and strong sunlight. Because plants are grown in containers regular attention to watering is required. The compost needs to be kept moist during summer but not continually saturated in winter, especially when there is a risk of it freezing and damaging the roots of plants such as shrubs and small trees that remain in the same container throughout the year. Nevertheless, such is the dedication and enthusiasm of many gardeners that roof gardens become enviable parts of city and town living.

Courtyards and patios are popular features in most gardens, whatever their size and shape. There, plants can be grown in containers as well as in borders surrounding them. Many plants grow immediately around the edges of patios and these include bedding plants for spring and summer displays, as well as special rose bushes which have a small stature but become smothered in flowers.

Borders

There are ideas to please everyone, and an early chapter is devoted to planning a flower border, and the selection of plants that will give an assured and long display. There are border suggestions for traditional cottage gardens, with their wide range of plants set in a casual and relaxed manner, borders for winter interest, and rose borders, the epitome of English gardens and a source of scent and colour throughout much of summer.

Water gardens

Water gardening is popular and usually a pond can be fitted into the smallest of gardens. Indeed, a formal pond set within a patio and with a small fountain creating a gentle and repetitious background sound can be a feature that is sure to capture attention. If more space is available, a bog garden positioned alongside an informal pond enables a wide range of moisture-loving plants to be grown in a relaxed and casual manner. Water features often entice damselflies and dragonflies into a garden; they hover and flit over the water's surface and help to bring further interest to a garden.

Tranquillity in gardens

There are many occasions, such as when children are small, active and rumbustious, when a garden has an 'all-action' nature. There are other times, however, when a peaceful and restful garden is more important in an attempt to ease the stress and tensions of modern living. Gardens – or even just parts of them – can be planned to be oases of rest and contentment. For many gardeners, a cool, shaded area is the epitome of a relaxed garden, while others appreciate the often comforting fragrances of scented plants, which can sometimes conjure up memories of holidays in exotic countries. Other plants, such as lilac and lilies, may aid the recall of wedding bouquets.

Meadow gardens have a restful nature, especially in spring and early summer, while a Zen garden reveals a calming nature throughout the year.

In this book you'll find the information and the inspiration you need to achieve all of these gardens.

plants for all types of garden

The range and styles of flower borders is impressively large and this chapter leads gardeners through the planning of them to the selection of suitable plants. Cottage gardens have an irresistible appeal, especially to gardeners who yearn for earlier times when vegetables, fruit trees and flowers flourished side-by-side in the same border. Other designs include winter-flowering borders that will capture and retain your attention during the long winter months. Rose gardens are also treasured features.

designing a cottage garden

The cottage garden evolved as a means of growing as many flowers, vegetables, fruits and herbs as possible in a small space. Everything is jumbled up together, so this style is not for the tidy-minded. Cottage gardens are colourful and charming, especially in the spring and summer when they come into their own.

▲ *The established hedges are worth maintaining in this otherwise under-exploited country plot.*

GARDEN DATA

location:	▦ West Country
climate:	▦ mild
soil type:	▦ chalk/clay
direction:	▦ west facing
aspect:	▦ open farmland

The brief

This small, west-facing, country garden has great views of open farmland and often spectacular sunsets. It already has useful, dense, boundary hedges to protect it from cold winds and the garden has plenty of sun, but the border beneath the hedge on the south side stays shady and cool until the afternoon. The owners love the idea of a traditional flower garden mixed with a few vegetables. They are young and fit and don't mind the physical work entailed in managing their new plot.

The design solution

We stripped a central area of existing turf, used a non-residual spray to kill germinating weed seedlings and then dug in loads of eco-compost to enrich the soil. We then covered this area of the garden with a layer of washed pea shingle – this will help keep weeds down and make them easier to remove. A path of wooden railway sleepers set in the remaining

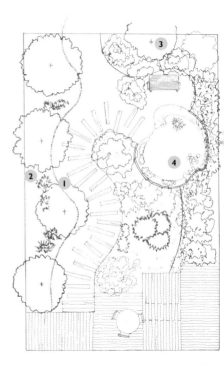

– 20 m x 9 m / 65 ft x 28 ft –

lawn connects the different areas of the garden. No cottage garden should be without at least one fruit tree, and for additional structure we included hazel wigwams to support climbing annuals and vegetables. A small wildlife pond is a surprise element in a sunny, tucked away spot.

▶ *A Victoria plum tree provides summer fruits.*

plum tree

pond

▲ *An informal pond benefits the ecosystem.*

bulbs

▲ *A variety of spring bulbs planted in the grass.*

path

▲ *Sleepers can be embedded in shingle or in turf to form a path.*

plants for a cottage garden

The cottage garden is at its best in spring and summer, brimming with flowering spring bulbs, summer annuals and seasonal perennials. Herbs, fruit and vegetables among the flowers are an essential part of the look. Choose ornamental forms whenever you can. Evergreens give structure, shape and winter interest.

Cottage garden flowers

An area of rough grass planted with bulbs adds charm to the cottage garden. For a natural look, scatter the bulbs on the ground and plant them where they fall. Choose a spot beneath a deciduous tree or shrub so that the crocuses, daffodils and other spring bulbs can get the light they need at flowering time.

Herbaceous perennials play a key role in cottage garden planting, with annuals sown or planted out in patches in between. The annuals will self-seed in places where they feel at home and the perennials will quickly form large clumps which can be divided in spring or autumn to make more plants. Plants grown close together soon get hungry. Winter gives you the opportunity to mulch the soil with well-rotted farmyard manure or your own garden compost to feed the perennials and keep the soil in good heart.

▶ Rosa gallica *is an ancient medicinal plant.*

Small trees and shrubs

A small fruit tree makes an ornamental and useful focal point which will also provide perching places for songbirds. Half-standards (with a clear, short length of stem below the branches) are on the right scale. Attracting wildlife is part of the garden's appeal so use shrubs such as buddleia to draw the butterflies, or plant a pyracantha to feed and shelter the birds, especially in winter.

Profile plants

Aster novi-belgii 'Apple Blossom'
MICHAELMAS DAISY 'APPLE BLOSSOM'

Michaelmas daisies help to extend the life of the garden well into the autumn and like all good cottage garden perennials they quickly make generous clumps. 'Apple Blossom' is a soft, old-fashioned pink and is particularly vigorous and hardy. No staking is needed, but the

plant may need to be sprayed to
control powdery mildew.

ht 75cm/30in

sp 45cm/18in

Soil and situation

Very undemanding as to soil. Best in
a light and sunny position but will
flower even in semi-shade.

Foeniculum vulgare 'Rubra'
RED FENNEL

Tall, feathery-leaved fennel is a
wonderful adornment and a traditional
cottage garden herb. Red-, bronze-
or purple-leaved forms lend a touch
of distinction. All have flattened
umbels of yellowish flowers which
add to the plant's delicate architecture
and attract beneficial hoverflies to the
garden. 'Rubra' is a red-leaved form.

ht to 1m/3ft

sp 45cm/18in

Soil and situation

Shaded, well-drained garden soil.

Rosa gallica
FRENCH OR PROVINS ROSE

This is the apothecary's rose of
ancient origin, whose purplish-
crimson flowers yield the best rose
oil. It needs little pruning and is small
and compact enough for small-scale
gardens. Use it to add height in
mixed planting.

ht 90cm–1.2m/3–4ft

sp 90cm/3ft

Soil and situation

Fertile, well-drained soil in sun.

▲ *Currant bushes provide vitamin-rich fruits.*

▲ *Fennel has aromatic, feathery leaves.*

SUITABLE PLANTS

Perennials

Centranthus ruber (valerian)

Dianthus (pinks), such as 'Dad's Favourite',
'Gran's Favourite', 'London Delight', 'Mrs
Sinkins', 'Prudence'

Geranium (cranesbill), such as 'Johnson's Blue'
and *G. renardii*

Heuchera (alum root), such as *Heuchera
cylindrica* 'Greenfinch', 'Palace Purple'

Lupinus polyphyllus Russell hybrids (Russell
lupin)

Nepeta (catmint), such as 'Souvenir d'André
Chaudron' (syn. 'Blue Beauty')

Paeonia officinalis (cottage garden peony)

Phlox (phlox), such as *Phlox paniculata*
'Amethyst' (pale lilac), 'White Admiral' (white)
and 'Windsor' (deep carmine pink)

Primula florindae (giant cowslip)

Pulmonaria (lungwort), such as *Pulmonaria
officinalis* 'Mawson's Blue' or *P. o.* 'Sissinghurst
White'

Scabiosa (scabious), such as *Scabiosa caucasica*
'Clive Greaves'

Verbena bonariensis

Annuals and biennials

Alcea rosea (syn. *Althaea rosea*) (hollyhock),
such as 'Chater's Double' or 'Majorette'

Aquilegia (aquilegia, columbine, granny's
bonnets), such as *A. flabellata* (soft blue),
A. longissima (pale yellow flowers, very long
spurs), *A. vulgaris* 'Nora Barlow' (extra frilly)
and Mrs Scott Elliott Hybrids (mixed colours)

Calendula (calendula, pot marigold) such as
Calendula officinalis 'Lemon Queen' or *C. o.*
'Orange King'

Centaurea cyanus (cornflower)

Clarkia elegans (clarkia)

Cosmos bipinnatus Sensation Series (cosmea)

Dianthus barbatus (sweet william)

Digitalis purpurea (foxglove)

Erysimum cheiri (wallflower)

Helianthus annuus (sunflower), such as 'Giant
Yellow' and 'Music Box'

Lathyrus odoratus (sweet pea)

Meconopsis cambrica Welsh poppy

Nigella damascena (nigella, love-in-a-mist)

Papaver rhoeas Shirley Series (shirley poppy)

Papaver somniferum (opium poppy)

designing a rose garden

Roses evoke the quintessential character of the classic Edwardian, English garden. Their glorious colours and scents and exquisitely shaped, velvety blooms provide universal inspiration for poetry, painting and music and they are coveted by gardeners all over the world.

▲ *This sheltered garden offers the ideal site for a range of roses. It receives enough sun and has good soil.*

GARDEN DATA

location:	▦ Wales
climate:	▦ mild/temperate
soil type:	▦ chalky clay
direction:	▦ south facing
aspect:	▦ open

The brief

This slightly sloping plot is sunny and sheltered from prevailing winds. The owners have long wanted a rose garden in the romantic style and accept that their garden will be at its most attractive in summer, rather than year-round. There is plenty of support for climbers and ramblers but the garden needs a central focal point and a clearly defined ground pattern, to draw attention away from the square outline shape.

The design solution

The garden is within a modern development and we decided on a contemporary approach rather than traditional, quartered or otherwise geometrically-shaped beds. We made use of the existing boundary fences and wigwams for climbers and ramblers and grouped shrub and ground cover roses around these schematically by colour. We also introduced plants that associate well with roses and some that will

– 22 m x 12 m/72 ft x 40 ft –

provide structure during the dormant months of winter. We used log roll to edge and retain the rose beds. Grass and brick look well with roses and we have used these traditional materials for surfaces and paths, making sure that the beds and borders are accessible for rose-sniffing, cutting and pruning.

log roll

Log roll makes an effective ▲
edging for planting beds.

gazebo

▲ A metal gazebo and
statue, or a fountain, can
provide the central feature.

rose

▶ 'Miss Alice' is a
dramatic rambler.

plants for a rose garden

There is a huge choice of roses, with a few for even the most difficult situations. A rose garden is a long-term creation so it pays to choose carefully. Check before buying that the rose's size and way of growing really are what you want. Visit rose gardens during the summer and consult specialist growers' catalogues.

Making preparations

Roses respond to good care even though they often thrive in polluted city air (its acidity deters mildew and black spot). They like a rich, heavy but well-drained soil, and as they are going to stay put the ground has to be well prepared for them. At least a month before planting dig the whole garden really well and work in as much manure as you can lay your hands on at the lowest level of the dug area. This will help to lighten heavy soils and give bulk to sandy soils as well as feeding the roses. It's best to plant in autumn from fresh stock, so prepare beforehand.

Planting bare-root roses

Before planting soak the roots in a bucket while you dig a deep hole wide enough to accommodate the spread-out roots. Mix crumbly soil with bonemeal, and garden compost if you have it, and add to the bottom of the hole. Sit the rose in, with the bulge called the union at the base of the stem just below the surface, fan out the roots and support the rose as you trickle in more soil, tucking it in round the roots as you go. Tread in and water well.

Care and maintenance

Roses need mulching, pruning, spraying and deadheading. Get hold of farmyard manure if you possibly can, and give each plant a deep mulching in the autumn and again in spring. Repeat-flowering roses need an extra feed in mid-summer. (You can use a proprietary rose feed for this.) Pruning is generally done in winter or early spring, and it's best to check on the requirements for each plant. Prevent mildew and black spot by spraying in early spring, and again

◄ R. 'Suffolk' makes excellent ground cover.

◄ *'Wedding Day' is a dramatic rambler.*

long period and produce bright orange-red hips.

ht 50cm/18in

sp 1.2m/4ft

Rosa 'Wedding Day'

'Wedding Day' is a light and airy rambling rose that will soon ramble over a shed or large arch or cover a pergola. It flowers very prolifically, the apricot buds opening to creamy yellow and quickly turning white. The flowers are single with a boss of bright yellow stamens.

ht and sp to 9m/30ft

Rosa 'Gertrude Jekyll'

This is a strong-growing and disease-resistant English rose (a recently developed breed of shrub roses with all the charm of old roses). Its fragrant, rosette-shaped flowers are a rich pink and it has a 'true rose' scent. The shrub can be pruned annually to half its size, and this will produce the biggest flowers.

ht 1.2m/4ft

sp 1m/3ft 6in

throughout the flowering season depending on how prone the plant is. Look out for aphids (greenfly and blackfly). Spraying with an appropriate insecticide may be necessary but diluted washing-up liquid often does the trick just as well. During the flowering season snip off dead flowers to encourage repeat flowering but remember to leave a final flush of flowers to produce hips in the autumn.

Profile plants

Rosa 'Suffolk'

This is a ground-cover rose, a low-growing, dense and bushy shrub with large sprays of bright scarlet flowers on arching stems, which make it suitable for planters as well. The gold-stemmed flowers are produced for a

► Rosa *'Gertrude Jekyll' is rich pink.*

designing a flower border

A stunning herbaceous border has long been seen as a pinnacle of gardening achievement. But this traditional form of border was originally designed to be at its best for only a few short weeks when wealthy families visited their country houses for the summer. Today we want interest from our gardens all year round.

▲ *This sloping garden offers huge potential for growing both sun- and shade-loving plants, so we schemed the borders accordingly.*

GARDEN DATA

location:	Midlands
climate:	mild/temperate
soil type:	chalky
direction:	east facing
aspect:	open

The brief

This long, east-facing garden slopes steeply upwards from the house. A shed and an elderly summer house are to be replaced and an old apple tree, awkwardly positioned in the centre of the lawn, moved. One long boundary is shady while the other is warm and sunny, so each border will have a very different planting plan, although each will cross-refer to the other by colour or form of plant. The view also needs to be restricted at intervals, so that you are keen to discover what lies beyond.

The design solution

The existing layout was reshaped to form two areas of unequal size, to avoid splitting the garden into two exact halves. Within these two areas we repositioned the potting shed and made a feature of the summer house. The planting is vibrant and hot on one side and cool and lush on the other, moving from traditional English herbaceous plants near the main house to exotic jungly leaves near the summer house. The lawn is unbroken by paths as its steep slope allows good drainage to gullies.

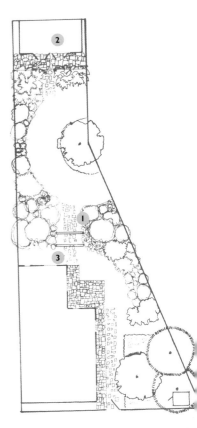

— 28 m x 15 m/90 ft x 50 ft

path

▲ *You can choose a path of single slabs, or a mosaic of smaller, adjoining stones.*

arch

summer house

▲ *The old summer house was replaced.*

▲ *A metal arch was installed for climbers.*

plants for a flower border

With border planting, it's the overall effect that matters, even though of course seeing individual plants at close quarters is part of the pleasure of growing them. Small is beautiful — a limited number of plants well used is much more effective than too many. Foliage makes a foil for flowers and can act as a link between groups.

▲ Hosta *'Whirlwind' provide strong shapes for a shady border.*

Planning and planting

As a general rule repeat planting creates rhythm and harmony, and planting in groups (massed planting) is much more effective than planting singly. At the same time, repeating at regular intervals is very dreary — varied repetition is what's called for. Bear in mind when planning the planting what the individual plant's eventual spread will be and don't be tempted to crowd too much in. You will need a few gaps for your feet when tending the plants, and bare patches can be filled with annuals or with plants in pots.

If you are starting from scratch you will need to prepare the border well before you plant, working in plenty of manure or other organic matter in the autumn. Although you can improve and control the growing conditions your garden offers to some extent, it's better to concentrate on plants that prefer the conditions you can offer in terms of soil, light, shelter and exposure than to aim at something which would be difficult to achieve. Most gardens offer at least two different aspects, so that there is a range of conditions to exploit, as long as plants with similar needs are grown together.

▶ Viburnum *'Opulus roseum', suits a sunny border.*

Brimming borders

Make the border as deep as you can – 1.5–2.5m/5–8ft, or more if you have the space – so that you can grow plants in bold clumps, with plenty of room at the front for smaller plants and space for shrubs, trees and climbing plants behind. As well as grading heights from front to back in this way, plan also for varying heights along the border, with taller groups at intervals. Choosing plants that are hardy will avoid disappointments, and if you select plants that need as little support as possible, or

◄ Calendula *'Pacific Beauty'*.

spring to prevent non-flowering, tangled growth.

ht to 5m/15ft

sp 1.5m/5ft

Soil and situation

Fertile soil, with its head in the sun and its feet in the shade.

plant them so that they can support each other, you will have less work to do. Don't be in too much of a hurry to tidy up when the autumn comes. Some plants look wonderful covered with winter frost or topped with a dollop of snow, and many seed heads are attractive, as well as providing food for birds.

Profile plants

Magnolia stellata

STAR MAGNOLIA

A starry-flowered magnolia of modest size and beautifully spreading habit, this is a gift for the border, although it will also stand alone in the lawn. It bears a multitude of fragrant, white, long-petalled flowers before the leaves in early to mid-spring. Spring-flowering bulbs such as scilla and crocus or cyclamen corms can flourish at its feet. It needs shelter from cold wind but is more robust than it looks.

ht to 3m/10ft

sp to 4m/12ft

Soil and situation

Fertile soil; light but sheltered position.

Heuchera cylindrica 'Greenfinch'

ALUM ROOT

The scalloped, mottled leaves of this heuchera form shiny mounds, above which stand tall, wiry stems carrying spikes of tiny lime-green flowers in stiff, airy panicles. An adaptable plant that's good for hot or cool borders, it flowers in early summer. Similar greenish-flowered heucheras include *H. c.* 'Chartreuse' and *H.* 'Green Ivory'

ht 90cm/3ft

sp 60cm/2ft

Soil and situation

Fertile soil that is well-drained but not too dry, in sun or partial shade.

Clematis 'Etoile Violette'

CLEMATIS

This is a viticella clematis with masses of small, nodding violet-coloured flowers from early summer right through to autumn. It is very pretty scrambling through a climbing rose, or over a yellow-leaved plant such as *Euphorbia polychroma* or a golden-leaved philadelphus. Another viticella hybrid is 'Abundance' with rose-pink flowers. Cut back each

designing a summer garden

A summer garden sacrifices year-round colour and structure in order to be at its glorious best for just a few months of the year. Sumptuous flowers and fragrances assail the senses only briefly, but provide memories of long summer days spent lazing in the garden that will sustain you through the dark winter evenings.

▲ *This small garden must exploit its natural attributes, brick walls and a strawberry tree, with the minimum expenditure.*

GARDEN DATA

location:	Wales
climate:	mild/temperate
soil type:	neutral
direction:	east facing
aspect:	open

Design brief

This tiny garden belongs to first-time home owners who are furnishing and decorating their home on a shoestring budget. It is an almost empty plot but has two valuable features: a 1.5m/5ft brick wall which, although neglected, encloses and shelters the garden, and a young *Arbutus unedo*, 'strawberry tree'. This beautiful tree is evergreen, has sensational, coppery, peeling bark, clusters of white, scented flowers and edible fruits. We recommend that in any summer garden you do not abandon evergreen planting altogether, because a large, bare patch of earth can look very dreary unless it is supported by some strong shapes of trees or shrubs.

Design solution

We chose very simple, geometric shapes that would allow the garden to be constructed as economically as possible. Unfussy lines define the broad flower borders without

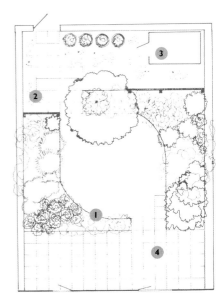

— 10 m x 7 m / 32 ft x 22 ft —

distracting from their show of colour. We used basic materials: regular sized, natural coloured paving slabs laid to exact measurements, to avoid cutting; tanalised timber trellis, and stone chippings to match the paving. The walls were re-pointed where necessary and coated with masonry paint in a shade of warm cream. The planting is in rich reds, yellows, oranges, creamy whites and blues, with silver-grey and green foliage.

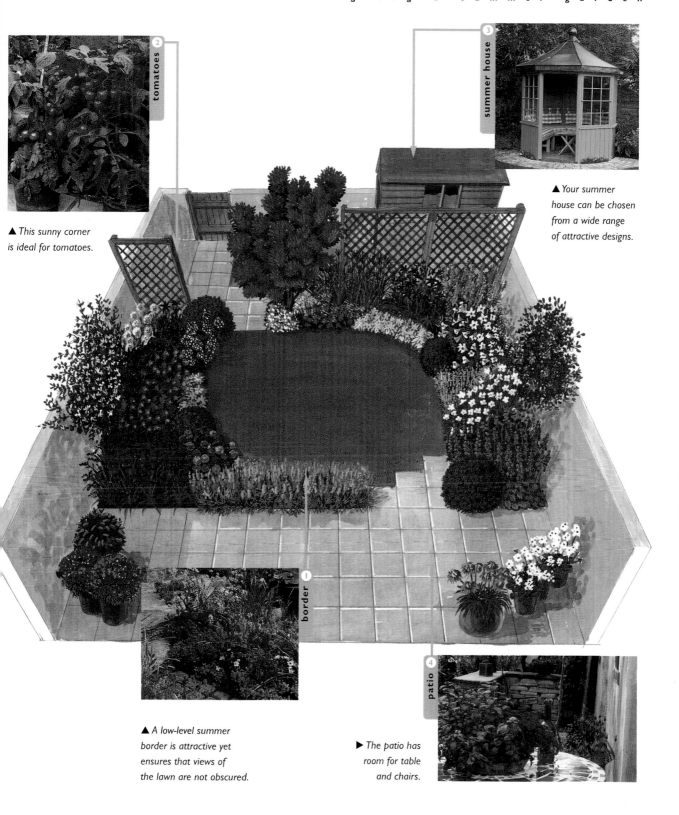

tomatoes

▲ *This sunny corner is ideal for tomatoes.*

summer house

▲ *Your summer house can be chosen from a wide range of attractive designs.*

border

▲ *A low-level summer border is attractive yet ensures that views of the lawn are not obscured.*

patio

▶ *The patio has room for table and chairs.*

plants for a summer garden

A large part of a summer garden will be used as an outdoor room. The aim is to make the surrounding areas a riot of colour – or a gentler haze, depending on the aspect and on your taste – to please the eye. Some permanent planting using shrubs, small trees or evergreens will help to give a more composed look.

Using summer colour

In full summer there are lots of hot or striking colours for drama and excitement in the garden. Strong reds, oranges and yellows look good in bright light and have a completely different effect when used together than when dotted lightly about. But the effect, though exciting and exotic, can be almost too strong unless you make contrasts, or use shades of green and plants with silver foliage to tone it down. For this reason it helps to have a lawn to act as green foil for a hot border. Green from foliage plants helps both to calm what might otherwise seem too bright and to make the transition between colours that don't look good side by side.

Annuals and bedding plants

Growing your own summer plants instead of buying them in trays from the garden centre or DIY superstore

◀ Crocosmia *'Lucifer'* is a real eye-catcher.

not only saves you money, it also gives you the chance to grow superior plants in colours of your choice instead of the standard mixtures. Petunias, impatiens (busy Lizzies), tobacco plants,

snapdragons, and many less familiar bedding plants, in our garden, can all be grown without much difficulty at all.

Annuals like the lovely opium poppy (*Papaver somniferum*) don't take kindly to being moved, and need to be sown where they are to grow, and others (including calendula or marigolds) are difficult to buy as plants yet incredibly easy to grow. Biennials such as the verbascums and sweet williams (*Dianthus barbatus*) in our garden are also quite easy to raise from seed. Pelargoniums can be tricky and are probably best raised from plugs (available from garden centres and by post).

▶ *The strawberry tree has attractive fruit.*

Profile plants

Crocosmia 'Lucifer'
MONTBRETIA OR CROCOSMIA

Crocosmias are summer flowers from corms, with flowers like miniature lilies in vibrant oranges and reds, and strappy green leaves, revealing their close kinship with irises. Originating from South Africa, crocosmia cultivars now grow in temperate climates all over the world. 'Lucifer' is a deep, bright, fiery red and will quickly form strong, healthy clumps that can be thinned in autumn if they get too big. Their normal height is at the lower end of the scale.
ht 1–1.5m/39in–5ft
sp 8cm/3in
Soil and situation
Crocosmias do well in any well-drained soil in a sunny position; they like heat and light but must not dry out completely.

Arbutus unedo
STRAWBERRY TREE

The strawberry tree is a rounded, evergreen shrub or small tree with reddish-brown bark and clusters of cream-coloured, waxy, bell-shaped, pendent flowers in autumn. The round, bumpy-surfaced fruits redden as they ripen. This takes a year, with fruits maturing as new flowers appear.

◀ *The long-spurred* Aguilegia longissima.

ht 4.5m/15ft
sp 3m/10ft
Soil and situation
Fertile garden soil, preferably, and a warm, sheltered position.

Aquilegia longissima
AQUILEGIA OR COLUMBINE

This elegant version of the country columbine, or old granny's bonnets, is a lovely pale lemon yellow, and the flowers have unusually long, bright yellow spurs. The flowers are fragrant and the leaves are delicate and ferny. Although it is strictly a perennial it is best grown as a biennial for fresh plants each year.

Aguilegia is fairly easily grown from seed, sown in the autumn.
ht 60–90cm/24–36in
sp 45cm/18in
Soil and situation
Well-drained soil, including poor soil, and a sunny situation.

designing a winter garden

A winter garden shows off structure, texture and form perhaps more than any other garden. The shapes of plants take on a mysterious beauty when rimmed with hoar frost, and you notice the extraordinary skeletons of seedheads and the delicate tracery of branches across a wintry sky.

▲ *Strong shapes, evergreens, and careful planning will be needed if this garden is to make an impact in winter.*

GARDEN DATA

location:	East Anglia
climate:	mild
soil type:	neutral
direction:	east
aspect:	open

The design brief

The owners of this traditional country cottage want their east-facing front garden to be at its best during the long winter months. Their sitting room overlooks the garden and they envisage cosy log-fire days during which they can observe and enjoy the garden from indoors, or wander out to feed the birds. The site is level and roughly triangular.

The design solution

The garden is shaded during the short winter afternoons but benefits from morning sunshine. To add colour we used old brick for the patio, although crazy paving or flagstones would be equally appropriate. We chose strong architectural shapes and some warm colours for the planting, which will be backlit by morning sunlight. The design adopts a more formal approach than we would employ for the larger and more private back garden. The layout counterbalances

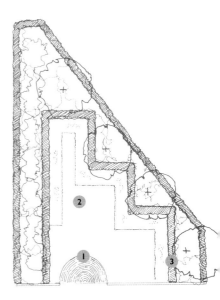

— 18 m x 14 m/58 ft x 46 ft —

the strongly triangular shape of the site and incorporates dramatically contrasting planting of tightly clipped evergreens with looser, breezy grasses and perennials. These are selected for their interesting seed heads, which are less likely to collapse in a mild and wet winter. We added a bird feeding station, positioned where it can be viewed from indoors.

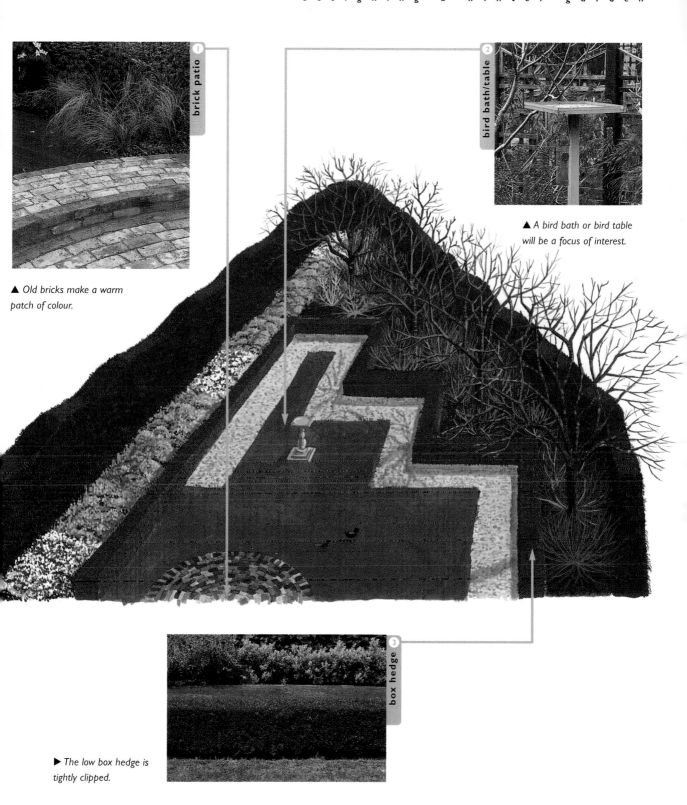

brick patio ①

② **bird bath/table**

▲ A bird bath or bird table
will be a focus of interest.

▲ Old bricks make a warm
patch of colour.

③ **box hedge**

▶ The low box hedge is
tightly clipped.

plants for a winter garden

There is plenty of glowing, sun-catching colour from bark, stems, and even leaves, for the winter garden, and almost all the winter-flowering shrubs have a wonderful fragrance as well as being surprisingly easy to grow. Most of them also provide excellent material for cutting for the house.

Flowers, bark and evergreens

Evergreens are a key feature of a successful winter garden. The formal design on pages 26–27 uses the classic box and yew, which clip neatly to shape. For a less formal garden the common laurel (*Prunus laurocerasus*) is excellent, shade-tolerant and vigorous, and garden birds often nest among its broad, leathery leaves. Various conifers, including gold, blue and pale green junipers, bring colour in winter, as well as contributing their interesting shapes, and the good old garden privet in green or gold (*Ligustrum ovalifolium* and *L.o.* 'Aureo-marginatum') is a useful standby for garden hedging.

Dogwoods (*Cornus*) and *Salix* species are outstanding for their winter stems, in reds and oranges, lively light browns, yellows and lime or olive green. Silver birches (*Betula* species) have pale silver-white or orange-red stems and the strawberry tree (*Arbutus unedo*) has bright, peeling, cinnamon-red winter bark. Many maples (*Acer* species), especially those known as the snakebark maples, are also grown for their bright, peeling winter bark. Fragrant flowers are part of winter's bounty, and these include the delicately perfumed snowdrop (*Galanthus nivalis*) and blue and purple-blue short-stemmed winter-flowering iris, *Iris reticulata*. (See the panel opposite for more examples.)

◀ Erica carnea *has excellent winter foliage.*

PLANTS FOR WINTER FRAGRANCE

- *Chimonanthus praecox* (syn. *C. fragrans*) (wintersweet) – bushy shrub with small, fragrant, brownish yellow, purple-centred flowers on bare stems; needs to be in a sheltered position
- *Daphne odora* (daphne) – woody evergreen shrub with small, very fragrant, purplish-pink winter flowers **Caution: the berries are poisonous**
- *Hamamelis mollis*; *H.* x *intermedia* 'Pallida' (syn. *H. m.* 'Pallida') (witch hazel) – well-shaped shrub with very fragrant, spidery, yellow flowers on bare branches
- *Lonicera fragrantissima* (honeysuckle) – semi-evergreen honeysuckle with creamy, scented winter flowers
- *Mahonia* x *media* 'Charity' (mahonia) – evergreen shrub with very fragrant yellow flowers and glossy green leaves (*Mahonia aquifolium* is similar but with denser heads of flowers)
- *Petasites fragrans* (winter heliotrope) – tall and spreading plant with dense clusters of scented greenish or yellowish flowers in rosettes of light green leaves
- *Viburnum farreri* (formerly *V. fragrans*), *V. grandiflorum* and *V.* x *bodnantense* 'Dawn' (winter-flowering viburnums) – all have small, pinkish white scented flowers

Profile plants

Buxus sempervirens
BOX

With its small and neat evergreen leaves and dense growth, box is a wonderful hedging plant for a low or medium hedge, as well as being *the* plant for topiary. Young plants 20–30 cm/9–12in high are used for hedges, planted 30–40cm/12–16in apart, and one-third of the growth must be clipped back in the first spring to encourage thick, bushy growth.

ht 3m/10ft unless clipped lower
sp to 1.8m/6ft
Soil and situation
Thrives in any ordinary garden soil in sun or partial shade.

Erica carnea
WINTER HEATH

Ericas are almost indistinguishable from heathers; this species has many named varieties which all make a wonderful display in winter, with masses of pink, purple, red or white flowers over the springy mounds of needle-like foliage. *Erica carnea* is a particularly useful species in that it will tolerate alkaline – chalky or limy – soils if given good drainage (most heathers sulk if not in peaty or acid soils). Among the many varieties to choose from, 'Aurea' is a gold-leaved form with pink flowers, and 'Vivellii' has bronze leaves and deep magenta flowers.

▶ *Hellebores have exquisite winter flowers.*

▶ *Salix alba 'Britzensis' has coloured stems.*

ht 30cm/12in
sp 60cm/24in
Soil and situation
Well-drained garden soil and a light position. Heavy soils can have sand dug in to lighten them.

Prunus serrula
FLOWERING CHERRY

This particular ornamental cherry is especially attractive in winter because of its shining, mahogany- or coppery-coloured, peeling bark. In spring it produces slim, willow-like leaves and clusters of small white flowers. The leaves turn yellow in autumn and the tree takes on a pleasing, rounded shape.

ht 8m/26ft
sp 5.5m/18ft
Soil and situation
Ordinary well-drained garden soil, preferably somewhat limy, and a light, open position. The tree should be staked until growth is well under way.

designing a seaside garden

Gardening by the sea can be a challenging task, but is less so if you create a basic design that does not try to compete with the elemental landscape of sea and sky. There are wonderful pieces of twisted bleached driftwood, shells and beach cobbles that can all find a place in your seaside landscape.

▲ This coastal site seems problematic but is easily turned into an attractive, low-maintenance garden.

GARDEN DATA

location:	▦ South Coast
climate:	▦ temperate
soil type:	▦ chalky
direction:	▦ west facing
aspect:	▦ open to seafront

Design brief

The L-shaped garden of this holiday home opens directly on to a shingle beach along part of its boundary and is exposed to salt-laden gales. Topsoil is virtually non-existent and is replaced by shifting shingle and sand. The garden needs a primary shelter belt and must be simply planted for low maintenance, as the owners visit only at weekends.

Design solution

We chose reclaimed oak planking for the deck and for the planked walkway towards the beach. An informal but sturdy fence is provided by similar oak planks inserted deeply into the shingle at varying heights. Lengths from old telegraph poles would do just as well. The 'fence' not only marks the boundary and helps break the force of the wind, but also helps anchor the shingle. We shaped the existing grass sward into a natural wave shape and added some large boulders for variety of texture.

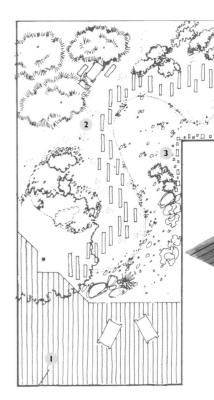

– 37 m x 10 m / 112 ft x 32 ft

Planting is strictly confined to a few low-maintenance species that can cope with the extreme conditions. These are grouped boldly around and between the boulders to form strong focal points.

decking

◀ *The sitting area is well sheltered from wind.*

windbreak

▲ *A windbreak can provide welcome protection from the elements.*

pea shingle

◀ *Cobbles and shingle mark a natural path to the beach.*

plants for a seaside garden

There are many plants for coastal areas. Despite the gales, at least the coastal climate is generally frost-free, and it may even be balmy. Most seaside gardens are exposed to high levels of sunshine and dry conditions from spring to autumn, so drought-tolerant, salt-wind-proof sun-lovers are generally required.

SHRUBBY PLANTS FOR COASTAL AREAS

Artemisia absinthium (wormwood) – mound-forming shrub with silvery-grey leaves
ht 90cm/3ft

Cytisus scoparius (common broom) – bright yellow flowers on bright green branches
ht to 2.5m/8ft

Escallonia species – glossy-leaved evergreen for warmer areas; white, pink or red flowers
ht 1.5–2.5m/5–8ft

Elaeagnus pungens – strong, evergreen shrub with glossy, green leaves and small but extremely fragrant cream-coloured tubular flowers in autumn

Fuchsia magellanica – hardy fuschsia with crimson and purple hanging flowers
ht 1.2–1.8m/4–6ft

Genista hispanica (Spanish gorse) – golden yellow flowers on tough, spiny branches
ht 60cm–1.2m/2–4ft

Olearia x *haastii* and *O. cheesmanii* (daisy bush) – evergreens with white flowers; glossy green leaves have white, felty backs
ht 1.8m/6ft; 3.6m/12ft (*O. cheesmanii*)

Juniperus communis (juniper) – weather-resistant evergreen (dwarf forms available)
ht to 3m/10ft

For plants for sunny, dry areas
see pages 40–41

Plants for the seaside

Plants for hot, dry, sunny places give away their sun-loving, or sun-tolerant nature partly by their leaves, as it's through its leaves that a plant loses moisture. To reduce water loss these plants have small or very narrow leaves, hairy leaves (as in silver- and grey-leaved plants) or waxy leaves. Succulent plants also are adapted to dry conditions, and this includes not only the true succulents (the cacti) but also fleshy-leaved plants such as sedums and houseleeks (*Sempervivum* species). Many flowering plants from bulbs and corms, such as the hardier agapanthus, alliums and crocosmia, can also do well by the sea, given some shelter.

Beating the wind

Wind-resistance is a key feature, as seaside places can suffer gales from autumn until late spring and strong

▶ *California poppies are bright and adaptable.*

winds even in summer. The solution is partly to provide shelter, but also to look out for wiry, spiky plants that sift the wind and resist water loss, and low-growing plants whose natural habitats are cliffs and rocks. Even a screen as low as 50cm/20in gives adequate shelter for low-growing plants, and plants themselves can form a screen. Phormiums, elaeagnus and several olearias (the daisy bush) – see panel opposite – all cope well.

Profile plants

Eschscholzia californica
CALIFORNIA POPPY

These brightly coloured but delicate looking poppy-like annuals are just right for grey pebbles and blue skies. California poppies love the sun and their petals close on cloudy days. They are very easily grown from seed, sown in succession from early spring onwards for a continuous display. The characteristic colour is orange, but mixtures with flowers in cream and yellow are available.

ht 20–30cm/8–12in

sp 10–15cm/4–6in

Soil and situation

Must have well-drained, poor soil (suitable for sandy and stony soils), and a sunny position.

▶ Rutus graveolens, *common rue.*

◀ *Flowers of the* Cynara cardunculus.

Cynara cardunculus
CARDOON

Related to the globe artichoke cardoons have the same statuesque, thistle-like magnificence, and these are very attractive plants with their woolly greyish-white stems, spiny grey leaves and purple thistle flowers which attract bees all summer long. Cardoons are best grown from seed. The leaf stalks and midribs can be blanched for eating.

ht 1.5m/5ft

sp 1.2m/4ft

Soil and situation

Well-drained, reasonably fertile soil in full sun, but with shelter from strong winds.

Ruta graveolens
COMMON RUE

Rue is a bushy herb with pretty blue-green leaves and small yellow flowers in summer. It was taken by the Romans to their colonies and is still an ingredient of the fiery Italian grappa. The leaves have a very distinct scent when crushed. It is used more as a decorative plant than as a culinary herb today. **Can cause blisters on sensitive skin.**

ht to 90cm/3ft

sp 75cm/30in

Soil and situation

This species is at its best in hot, dry places, in poor, well-drained or sandy soil and a sunny position.

designing a roof garden

A roof garden is the perfect get-away-from-it-all solution for city dwellers. Relatively private, it can be a pleasant retreat for weekend breakfasts, summer sunbathing or drinks parties – or it can be a simple space for a few containers positioned just outside a window where you can reach them for watering.

▲ *This small roof top needs work and a good safety rail, but its stunning view over farmland lends the area great potential.*

GARDEN DATA

location:	Cornwall
climate:	mild temperate
soil type:	n/a
direction:	north facing
aspect:	open roof tops

The brief

The offices of a small family-owned company are two floors above ground level in the centre of a busy seaside town. Although it's exposed to strong, salt-laden winds the staff decided to utilize this small flat roof as a garden space, to be enjoyed from inside the building and to add variety and interest to the views of the town roofscape and farmland beyond.

The design solution

We chose tough, woven, polythene netting to form a perfect lightweight windbreak that allows light through to the plants but protects them from strong winds. A 'crazy log' floor makes a perfect decorative surface for this roof and lets air circulate beneath the containers. Galvanized buckets make great planters – we drilled holes for drainage, painted the buckets the steely blues and greens of the nearby sea and grouped them around the roof space. They were then planted with phormiums,

– *9 m x 4 m / 30 ft x 12 ft* –

eryngiums, sea kale, easy-care grasses to catch the breeze, and sedums. We set the containers amongst scattered white beach cobbles. For summer flowering we included white pelargoniums, and for fun you could add a windsock or flag.

galvanized buckets 2

▲ *Plastic or galvanized buckets make smart and lightweight containers.*

artificial turf 1

▲ *Artificial turf provides light, hard-wearing flooring.*

plants for a roof garden

A roof top site is likely to be exposed to every kind of weather. So, even with a windbreak, a choice of resilient plants will be a priority. The roof will probably be open to the sun too, so include some sun-lovers and plants such as grasses, which respond beautifully to breezes on sunny days.

Plants for sun and wind

Resourcefulness is required when planting a roof garden. You want to make the most of what is usually a small and inaccessible space and you are likely to want low-maintenance

◀ Eryngium x oliverianum, *sea holly*.

plants so that you can spend more time sitting in the garden than tending plants. Whatever you choose it's as well to accept from the outset that you will probably have to replace more plants here than in any other type of garden.

Many herbs enjoy an open, light and sunny spot. Thymes, lavenders and rosemary in particular thrive in such a position. Plants for dry and well-drained soils, including some grasses, broom or gorse, are also ideal. Plants that are too tall will catch the wind except in a sheltered corner so it's best to choose lower-growing varieties rather than risk top-heavy plants toppling over (light grasses, however, such as *Stipa gigantea*, should be safe as the wind is filtered through them). The best way to make variations in height is to use planters of different sizes, or put them on stepped stands, and these should be placed mainly around the roof edges

unless you are sure the structure is sound enough to bear the weight of pots placed centrally.

SUITABLE ROOF PLANTS

Allium flavum – low-growing, yellow, summer-flowering allium ht 30cm/12in

Buddleia davidii varieties (buddleia) – arching branches of honey-scented, purple flowers ht to 3m/10ft

Crambe maritima (sea kale) – low-growing with thick, bluish leaves ht 75cm/30in

Kniphofia (red hot poker) – tall torches of red, orange or yellow flowers ht 90cm–1.8m/3–6ft

Santolina chamaecyparissus (cotton lavender) grey-green mounds with buttony yellow flowers ht 50cm/20in

Pleioblastus pygmaeus var. *distichus* (pigmy bamboo) – short, very leafy green bamboo ht to 90cm/3ft

Sedum spectabile (sedum or ice plant) – fleshy, grey-green foliage and pink flowers ht 45cm/18in

Stipa gigantea (giant feather grass) – arching feathery flowers above architectural leaves ht 1.8–2.5m/6–8ft

See also plants for seaside gardens, pages 32–33

▶ Pennisetum alopecuroides *'Hamelin'*.

Profile plants

Eryngium × oliverianum
ERYNGIUM

Eryngiums or sea hollies are excellent plants for a roof garden as their architectural, branching stems filter the wind and the spiky bracts which surround their cone-shaped flower heads look good in strong light. *Eryngium × oliverianum* has particularly frosted-looking stems, bracts, leaves and flowers in silvery blue, sometimes purple-tinted. It flowers during the whole summer.

ht 90cm/3ft

sp 45cm/18in

Soil and situation

Poor, well-drained soil, sunny situation.

Pennisetum alopecuroides varieties
FOUNTAIN GRASS

These grasses have many varieties suitable for roof tops because of their dense, low, mound-forming growth and undemanding nature. The feathery bottle-brush flowers rustle over narrow arching leaves all summer. In 'Hamelin', a compact form, the flowers begin in early summer and the leaves become golden yellow in autumn as the flowers turn from white to a soft greyish brown. 'Bunny' is another variety to look out for.

ht 60cm–1.5m/2–5ft

sp 60cm–1.2m/2–4ft

Soil and situation

Light, well-drained but fairly fertile soil, in a sunny situation.

◀ Phormium tenax, *a hardy, strong plant.*

Phormium species
PHORMIUM

Given a sunny, warm situation phormiums are tough as old boots and there are several good, smaller species of this striking architectural plant. *Phormium cookianum* is the mountain flax, normally with yellowy green colouring, but the hybrid 'Maori Sunrise' has apricot and pink stripes and bronze outer edges to its leaves. The species *P. tenax* itself is something of a giant, but 'Bronze Baby' is a dwarf hybrid with bronze–coloured leaves which turn downward at the tips. 'Dazzler' has leaves striped red, orange and pink.

ht and sp to 2m/6ft;

75cm/30in 'Bronze Baby'

Soil and situation

Well-drained but fairly fertile soil in a sunny situation.

designing a patio garden

A front patio makes an instant statement about a house and its owners. It is the setting in which visitors first view the house and welcoming area. It is also usually less private than the back garden and should therefore be simply designed, in harmony with the style and materials of the house, secure and easily maintained.

▲ *This front patio garden leaves much to be desired, especially as there is no back garden to compensate.*

GARDEN DATA

location:	Northern Ireland
climate:	temperate
soil type:	neutral
direction:	east facing
aspect:	partially shaded

The brief

This small space, bounded by low brick walls, typifies the size of many front gardens on housing estates. In this instance the developers have used cheap materials and mixed several different colours, shapes and textures together to make an uninspired and unwelcoming garden, which does not relate at all to the attractive mews-style house it fronts. Although there is not much of it, the existing planting is unharmonious and out of scale with the house. As there is no back garden this tiny area must double for its owners as somewhere to sit and relax.

The design solution

We liked the grey stone setts that are used to pave the private roadway to this small development and decided to echo them by using similar small unit setts to replace the existing concrete slabs. Instead of paving wall to wall we left a generous border for planting and varied the surface

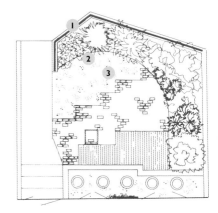

— 7 m × 6 m / 22 ft × 19 ft —

texture by introducing creamy white stone chippings. These also define the shape of the paved area. Close to the house we laid a timber deck, which provides a small seating area bounded by bright-coloured plants in containers. In colder weather it can be used as a stage for winter-flowering violas and heathers in carefully grouped containers. We erected neat, timber, picket fencing along the front boundary wall, to afford some privacy without casting dense shade. The planting is simple – fragrant, white flowering climbers and lush, leafy, evergreen foliage, with vivid splashes of hot colour.

fence

hostas

chippings

▲ Planting helps create privacy.

▶ Hostas thrive in a shady area.

▶ Stone chippings complement the pale paving.

plants for a patio garden

For a good-looking, low-maintenance patio that enhances the house invest in the building and construction, choosing the best materials you can afford, in keeping with the house. Then invest some more in long-lived, evergreen plants that will give shape and interest throughout the entire year.

Plants for form and flowers

Even in a sunny patio, a choice of evergreen shrubs will provide you with shaded areas, and an underplanting of shade-loving plants such as the leafy hostas (see page 69) and ferns (see pages 58–59), and winter- or spring-flowering hellebores will fit the bill nicely. Foxgloves *(Digitalis purpurea)* will self-seed in semi-shade, while patches of lady's mantle can spill over on the hard surfacing in sunny areas.

Summer-flowering plants, such as pelargoniums or nasturtiums grown from seed, can be grown in pots near the house for shelter and ease of care, and climbing plants such as clematis and jasmine can be grown on trellis up the walls of the house. Most patios will get plenty of sun (or you wouldn't choose to have them where they are) and there are many plants that thrive in these conditions. Plants for roofs and seaside gardens will be suitable for sunny patios too (see pages 32–33 and 36–37).

Profile plants

Choisya ternata
MEXICAN ORANGE BLOSSOM

This is a very glossy evergreen shrub with beautifully scented small white flowers over a long period in late spring and throughout summer, giving it the appearance and fragrance of an orange tree in blossom. The leaves release a pleasant aromatic scent when crushed. Preferring warmth and shelter, but extremely tolerant and needing little or no pruning, these are excellent plants for providing year-round structure and interest. A golden-leaved cultivar, 'Sundance', is also available.

◀ Choisya ternata, *Mexican orange blossom.*

ht to 1.8m/6ft

sp to 2.5m/8ft

Soil and situation

Ordinary, well-drained garden soil, and a position in sun or partial shade. In colder areas choisya does best

against a sheltering wall. Cutting off any frost-damaged shoots in spring encourages new shoots to grow.

Mahonia × media 'Charity'
MAHONIA

The mahonias are useful low-maintenance plants well suited to a patio garden and rewarding anyone who plants them with lily-of-the-valley-scented flowers in winter or early spring, depending on the variety. 'Charity' flowers all winter, with long racemes of small yellow flowers in plentiful bunches. Glossy, dark-green, rather holly-like leaves make the plant attractive when it's not in flower, and blue-black berries follow on from the flowers.

ht to 3m/10ft

sp to 2.5m/8ft

Soil and situation

Although tolerant, mahonia prefers humus-rich, moisture-retaining soil and a position in light shade; the plant will brave some wind and winter exposure.

▶ *Winter-flowering* Mahonia × media *'Charity'.*

◀ Ilex aquifolium *'J.C. van Tol'.*

Ilex aquifolium 'J.C. van Tol'
HOLLY

When choosing a holly tree for a small garden you need one that is shapely, not too large, and self-fertile so that it will produce berries without a partner. 'J.C. van Tol' is obliging in all these respects and is particularly generous with its bright red berries. It has smooth, beautifully glossy leaves from dark purple stems and a variegated variety, 'Golden van Tol', with yellow-edged leaves is also available. The tree is slim in shape and very hardy, so that it can be used to provide shelter for less robust plants.

ht 3–5.5m/10–18ft

sp 1.8–3m/6–10ft

Soil and situation

Ordinary garden soil, preferably with some moisture, and any position, in sun or shade. The variegated form needs sun for best colouring. Tolerates polluted city air.

designing a courtyard garden

A courtyard garden is at its most elegant when it follows clean contemporary lines, with sleek modern furniture. But if you prefer a traditional look you can fill it with pots and containers, and cover the walls with climbers. Paving, tiles and shingle make the surfaces, and your containerized plants can be changed to suit your mood.

▲ *Contrary to first impressions this dark, overgrown courtyard offers surprising possibilities for a major transformation.*

GARDEN DATA

location:	▪▪ North East
climate:	▪▪ mild/temperate
soil type:	▪▪ chalky clay
direction:	▪▪ north facing
aspect:	▪▪ urban enclosed

The brief

This tiny space is dark and shady because of long-neglected boundary plants that have grown out of control. The owner is not a keen gardener but would like some variety of colour and interest through the year, and would like to use the courtyard as an extra summer room for relaxing and entertaining friends.

Courtyards on the north or east side of the house will be cool and shady whereas those that face south can be real suntraps. When planning a courtyard garden the first thing to do is to decide how it will be used – somewhere to sit and soak up the sun, a quiet place or a social area.

The design solution

The area was cleared wall to wall to maximize space and light and the dilapidated fencing was replaced with colour-stained screening trellis to allow light to filter through but retain privacy. Small spaces work best if they are not too busy, so we

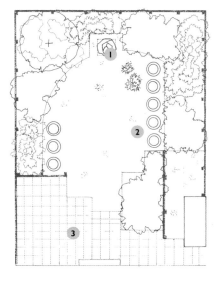

— 7 m x 9 m/22 ft x 30 ft —

chose unfussy paving to replace the dark, brick patio and combined it with creamy shingle to reflect as much light as possible. Planting is bold and simple, with splashes of colour provided by containerized annuals that can be replaced each year. We installed automatic irrigation and one uplight to make a dramatic focal point of the owner's beautiful piece of contemporary sculpture.

sculpture

▲ You can choose from a variety of
garden sculptures.

pots

▲ Matching containers
always look stylish.

paving

◀ A paved patio provides an unfussy seating area.

43

plants for a courtyard garden

Small enough to take in at a glance, courtyard gardens offer special opportunities for planting. Planting within the courtyard will usually be in containers or raised beds, while the boundaries can be used to great effect, with hedging plants if you want a 'live' boundary or climbing plants to cover walls or trellis.

A courtyard theme

For the best effect stick to a strong scheme, even if you want the effect to be exotic, dramatic or riotous. Too much going on in a small place will otherwise risk looking muddled. Use containers that are similar in style, whether it's brightly painted buckets,

◀ Yucca filamentosa *in flower.*

old stone troughs or Versailles planters. Have a strong theme for plants and don't use too many 'highlight' plants – one glorious flowering climber given prominence can be more successful than several in uneasy competition.

Container plants
for a sunny courtyard

A sunny courtyard, if also well sheltered, can be host to the most exotic plants. The following can all be grown as striking specimens in large containers in a Mediterranean-style courtyard. All need rich, easy-draining compost.

Agapanthus 'Blue Giant': drumheads of blue flowers on tall stems, broad, strappy leaves
ht 1.2m/4ft
sp 60cm/2ft

Ensete ventricosum (syn. *Musa ensete*): banana-like plant from Ethiopia with enormous leaves in bright olive

green and huge bronze and white flowers
ht to 6m/20ft
sp to 4.5m/15ft

Hakonechloa macra 'Aureola': golden-leaved, mound-forming grass – smaller than most grasses - looks stunning in a container
ht 35cm/14in
sp 40cm/16in

Musa basjoo: a banana plant from Japan with long rippled leaf blades and exotic brown and yellow flowers followed by inedible fruit
ht to 4.5m/15ft
sp to 3.6m/12ft

Phormium tenax (New Zealand flax): clump-forming plant with tall, architectural, strappy leaves and even taller stems of dark red flowers
ht 3m/10ft (leaves), 3.6m/12ft (flowers)
sp 1.8m/6ft

Yucca filamentosa (Adam's needle): rosettes of sharply pointed leathery leaves and upright heads of small cream flowers
ht and sp 90cm/3ft

◄ *Parrot tulips have striking frilly flowers.*

small. Try some of these varieties:
Hedera colchica, 'Dentata' and *H.c*
'Dentata Variaegata': large
green/variegated, tooth-edged
leaves, vigorous growth
Hedera helix 'Eva': small lobed leaves
with creamy margins; modest growth
Hedera helix 'Maple Leaf': less
vigorous ivy with deeply serrated,
maple-like leaves

Climbers for warm courtyards

These plants will need support from
wires or trellis if grown up a wall.
All grow to 5m/16ft or more.
Clematis armandii: evergreen, scented,
cream-flowered early clematis
Clematis montana var. *rubens:* pink-
flowered version of the vigorous
early summer-flowering clematis

Lonicera periclymenum 'Serotina': late-
flowering, very fragrant honeysuckle
Passiflora caerulea (passion flower):
exotic, starry, crown-of-thorns
flowers in creamy white with purple-
blue markings
Rosa banksiae: pale yellow or white
clusters of slightly scented flowers in
early spring
Solanum crispum (Chilean potato
vine) 'Glasnevin': vigorous purple-
flowered jasmine-like climbing plant,
but with no scent
Vitis coignetiae grapevine whose leaves
colour a rich purple-red in autumn
(black grapes are not edible)

Ivies for shady walls

Green ivies are the perfect wall-
climbers for shady courtyards, and
need no support. Ivies with yellow
variegation prefer some sun. Many
leaf forms are available, large and

◄ Solanum crispum *is a vigorous climber.*

water gardens

A garden pond, rich in aquatic plants and with a fountain splashing water on the surface, is often the most treasured part of a garden. Early Islamic gardens used water to create a restful ambience, with the almost hypnotic and repetitive note of water splashing on water adding an enduring quality. Bog gardens enable a wide range of moisture-loving herbaceous perennials to be grown in gardens; try adding one to a side of an informal pond.

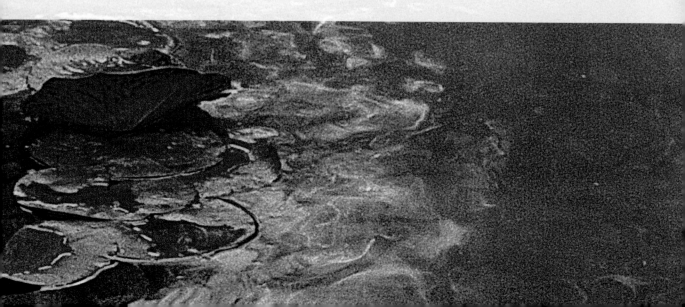

ponds and bog gardens

If you make a pond the dominant feature in the garden everything else can be designed to acknowledge it. All you will need is somewhere to sit and watch the water and a pathway from which you can observe the life of the pond at close quarters and enjoy all it has to offer.

Guidelines to design

Placing a pond requires some planning. First, a pond needs light and shelter. If the place for sitting and looking at it can be sited with the light falling from behind, it will enhance the pond experience. Once filled, the pond will be kept topped up by the natural rainfall in all but the driest weather, so a water supply is not vital. Choose an area not too close to the house and without overhanging trees – autumn leaves will decay in the water and make it smelly, and shade will cause algae and slime to gather on the water. Full sun is also to be avoided, except for a water lily pond, as this too encourages excessive growth of algae.

The best possible site is a hollow, or in a low level of the garden where you'd expect water to collect naturally. Make sure, however, that this is not a frost pocket where plants will fail to thrive, and not a place where the water table will rise higher than the lining of the pond. This will cause the liner to balloon in the middle and you will have an unwanted 'hippo' in your pond.

Style and size of pond

When it comes to choosing a garden pond, natural and informal are the key words for all but the grandest or most formal gardens. Make your pond as appropriately large as you can afford. Not only does it look better, but also the bigger the surface

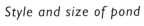

◄ *Moisture-loving plants for a bog or pond garden grow rapidly and are easy to maintain; they soon provide a lush, almost tropical look.*

◀ *Make sure you plant some marginal aquatics in the shallow reaches of the pond to soften the edges where it meets the bank.*

area the less likely it is to suffer from unwanted algae. Keep curves generous and unfussy and avoid a complete circle, which, like squares and rectangles, is suitable only for a formal setting. A kidney shape with a generously proportioned inner curve will look good and allow you to observe pond activity more easily. Modern flexible liners, used with a cushioning layer of underlay, are the best materials for such ponds. Don't forget that digging out a pond will create a lot of spoil, but rather than disposing of it, you may prefer to landscape the rest of the garden, and use the spoil from the pond to create undulations. Whatever you do, save any fertile topsoil for the planted areas.

▶ *This beautiful pond and water feature emulate a mountain stream. The margins are densely filled with bog and pond plants.*

Finishing details

Edge at least half of the pond with a damp garden, or bog area, where moisture-loving plants can grow and soften the outline. They will also provide shelter for wildlife. Include a shelf for marginal plants and a gently sloping shingle beach for small animals to climb in and out of the water. If possible allow for grass to run right to the edge of part of the pond, for a natural look.

If you plan to stock fish, your pond needs to be at least 90cm/3ft deep at the centre, in case the surface freezes in winter and so that the fish can hide away from predators. It's a bad idea to introduce ornamental 'koi' carp to a natural pond. They need a high quality filtration system and impeccably clean water with plenty of depth. They also need protection from herons, which, although beautiful birds, will wade in and enjoy delicious take-aways at your expense.

Wood and stone are natural companions to water, and decking in treated timber can extend over the pond so that you can stand above the water. A means of crossing the water, usually best located at the neck of the pond, can be used to add to the sense of flow and link the two sides of the pond visually as well as physically.

designing a bog garden

A constantly damp garden is often the result of badly drained surface water. There may be a heavy clay subsoil preventing drainage, or a hard, compacted surface where the soil has not been cultivated for many years, or the garden may be sited in a hollow which gathers the run-off rainwater from surrounding higher ground.

▲ A predominantly damp site is ideal for bog plants, most of which are lushly dramatic and will shelter a range of amphibian wildlife.

GARDEN DATA

location:	South coast
climate:	mild
soil type:	wet clay, slightly acid
direction:	east
aspect:	overlooks woodland

Design brief

This is a small garden with a high water table, which makes it difficult to site a pond. In consistently wet weather the pressure from held ground water will cause a pond liner to billow up like a hippo. However, the owners of the garden would like to encourage wildlife and are keen to make the most of their boggy ground. We need to bear in mind that the level of moisture will vary at different times of the year as the water table rises and falls.

Design solution

The answer is to go with the flow! We designed the garden informally, along curvy, natural lines, using timber planking for the decking and bridge and log rounds to form stepping stones in the grassy path.

The planting is equally informal and concentrates on several big, dramatic feature plants, interspersed with moisture-loving perennials and grasses. The larger plants form natural

− 13.5 m x 7 m / 43 ft x 23 ft −

barriers so that the whole garden cannot be seen from any one vantage point. The secrecy and intimacy that this kind of planting creates also provides hideaways for small and timid wild creatures.

log stepping stones ①

▲ Log rounds used as stepping stones.

iris ②

▲ Some irises require a wet situation.

plank bridge ③

◀ A simple plank over the pond.

water tank ④

▶ A recycled water tank houses a small lily.

5 1

plants for bog gardens

Natural-looking planting is best for an informal pond. There may be grasses rustling beside the water, irises wading in the shallows, a few water lilies floating in a still, sunny patch and streams of trailing plants waving in the water's depths. Water plants have a calming quality and attract wildlife to the pond.

Creating an effect

The plants around the pond form part of the whole scene. The huge leaves of gunnera (like giant rhubarb), ornamental willows and dogwoods with their brightly coloured winter stems, even small trees such as weeping willow, all add mood and atmosphere. Like the aquatic plants within the pond and the marginals at the water's edge they will be mirrored in the water.

Gently sloping banks offer the best hospitality to waterside plants. In a small pond the best way to obtain a slope at the right angle is to make a planting ledge around part of the edge. Do this by digging a wide and shallow step with an almost vertical slope at the back (up to the edge of the pond) and a steep drop down at the front into the pond's depth. The step is then filled with a raked slope of earth, retained by rocks and stones. Of course if the pond is large enough

▶ *The summer-flowering* Primula secundiflora.

the sides can slope gently from the edge down to the pond bottom.

Marginal planting area

Allowing the earth of a planting ledge to continue over the liner top, instead of bringing the liner right up and over the edge of the pond, means that the pond is not water-tight and you will have a damp area in which to grow beautiful if unpleasant sounding bog plants (or marginal plants). A piece of perforated liner extending on from the main liner

◄ *Pond grass:* Miscanthus sinensis *'Gracillimus'.*

can be used to line a shallow hollow dug out next to the pond, extending the pond into a larger bog area. This is then lined with a layer of gravel for drainage and filled with clean soil topped with gravel.

Planting in containers

You can plant directly into soil on your planting ledges, or decide to use hessian-lined planting containers filled with good clean soil and topped with 15mm/⅝in pea shingle. The hessian is then brought up and tied round the top to stop the soil leaking into the pond.

In the pond itself, water lilies are usually planted in special crates that are lowered to the bottom in stages so that their leaves are always floating. If the bottom is too deep, use crates or breeze blocks to make a platform. Submerged plants that oxygenate the water can be dropped

straight in. Their roots will grow downwards into the silty pond bed.

Choosing plants

Choose pond plants that are not too vigorous for the size of the pond, with plenty of oxygenating plants to help keep the water free of algae. It is better to have too many and have to remove some occasionally than too few. The planting scheme around the pond should not be too hectic. Areas of colour should be used against a background of green from foliage plants such as ferns, bamboos and grasses. Plants such as water irises give wonderful leaf shape as well as flowers and are naturally at home in a pond context. Most suppliers of aquatic plants are knowledgeable and can give good advice on suitable plants.

Profile plants

Miscanthus sinensis
MISCANTHUS

Grasses waving at the water's edge and whispering in the breeze are a key part of the planting in the pond garden. *Miscanthus sinensis* varieties have arching leaves and erect stems with plumes of silky flowerheads in late summer. *M. s.* 'Gracillimus' or maiden grass has very narrow leaves with white midribs and turns bronze

in autumn; *M. s.* 'Morning Light' is similar but with a silvery effect.

ht and sp 1.2m/4ft

Iris species
WATER IRIS

Water irises have a natural affinity with an informal pond. Their fanned, sword-shaped leaves, tall stems and inimitably graceful flowers are luscious to look at. *Iris pseudacorus* is the yellow flag iris – a true water iris that will grow with its feet in the water; *I. sibirica*, the Siberian iris, is blue or white, and requires rich, moist soil.

ht to 1. 2m/4ft or more

sp 90cm/3ft

▶ *Water iris is an easily-established bog plant.*

5 3

water gardens

For anyone who hasn't got the space or inclination for a pond there are many delightful ways of introducing water into the garden. 'Built-in' features are particularly at home in small-scale surroundings, whether in a small, enclosed garden or in a terraced area or patio close to the house.

◄ *This ornamental metal grid over a formal pond is also a safety feature that prevents children from falling into or playing in the pond.*

Fixed features

The advantage of simple moving-water features is that their installation involves very little work as there is no excavation, and no displaced earth to move. Many can be bought ready-made, though it has to be said that they're not always in the best taste. The ingenious can make their own, using a pump kit and a bit of DIY skill. Basically all you need is a sump, a pump, a pipe and a spout. The sump is the reservoir of water, which is pumped through the pipe to emerge from a spout – or simply from the concealed end of the pipe. The water returns to the reservoir and is continually recycled. The reservoir can be a bowl, basin or sink, forming part of the feature, or can be hidden away behind or beneath it; the spout can be anything from a huge old bath tap to an ornamental lion's-head, gargoyle or green man mask or a length of bamboo.

Moving-water features are often fixed to a wall, and therefore relatively safe even when there are young children about, but you should always bear safety in mind if you have a young family. If this is not a consideration, and you would rather have a still and silent feature for calm, serene contemplation, it is very easy to produce a miniature water lily pond in a watertight container. If you do this, however, don't think about adding even the smallest fish (the water could get much too hot in summer, and will freeze in winter). Ground-level features, such as fountains with water falling onto

▶ *The stone Buddha adds to the mood of contemplation created by the gentle sound of flowing water and simple planting.*

pebbles, may be safe for children as there is no depth of water, but even the smallest pool and fountain, with any water depth however shallow, would be inadvisable for unattended young children.

Discreet charms

Sometimes discretion is the better part of fixed water features. They are at home in shady positions, where they can gather moss. The sound should be restful not irritating, and not annoying to the neighbours. It becomes more muffled as the depth

of water in the receptacle increases: a depth of 25cm/10in or more creates a restful splash. The rate of flow and the height from which the water falls are also important (the faster and the higher, the noisier). Water falling onto stones creates a soothing splashing sound quite different from the sound of water on water. The wider the delivery pipe, the more restful the gurgle.

Adjusting the flow valve on the pump enables you to vary the rate of water flow. Make sure that the valve is accessible so that you can experiment until you get the visual effect – and sound – exactly to your taste. Art lies in concealment – the pump must not be visible, and preferably should not be audible.

◀ *This contemporary water feature comprises a series of stones. The sharp concrete edges are softened by the use of lilies and grasses.*

designing a water garden

Patios and terraces can often seem devoid of interest. One way of enlivening the space is to add a small, self-contained water feature. This will provide the soft and refreshing sound of water during lazy summer lunches al fresco and a theatrical night-time feature when carefully lit.

▲ *At present, the home and garden do not fully integrate. A water feature on the terrace echoes the stream along the boundary.*

GARDEN DATA

location:	East Anglia
climate:	cold/windy
soil type:	light clay
direction:	west facing
aspect:	sloping to trees

Design brief

This imposing Victorian home has a substantial width of terrace along the two sides of the house facing the garden. The garden slopes down and away from the house and so there is no feeling of the house nestling in its setting. The problem was to find a way of linking the building with the garden below.

Design solution

A stream runs along the far boundary at the bottom of the site and this provided the clue as to how to link house and garden. A water feature integral to the terrace would bring a natural element to the hard landscaping and echo the wilder parts of the garden below. The owners love to entertain and much of the level terrace space is taken up with tables and seating for large parties. An existing old brick wall at one end of the main terrace offered an ideal support for a wall-mounted fountain which would trickle into a reclaimed

– 6 m x 3 m/18 ft x 10 ft –

stone trough. This was set in stone chippings among random-sized crazy paving identical in colour and texture to the slabs on the existing terrace. By matching colours and textures we were able to move from formal terrace to informal water feature with the minimum of work and cost. The fountain is softened by the planting of large ferns, perennials, hostas, grasses and aquatic plants.

▲ Water spouts out of a
mounted lion's head into a
reclaimed stone trough.

▲ Waterproofed wooden barrels as
containers offer further scope for water plants.

▲ Asplenium ferns appreciate the moist, shady,
cool conditions found beside water.

masque

barrel

ferns

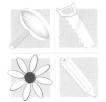

plants for a water garden

Lush and green are usually the keynotes for planting around a water feature, with ferns and mossy-looking plants enjoying the cool moisture. Exceptions apply to a water bubble, fountain or rill in a sunny courtyard or on the patio, where pots of spiky and exotic hot-weather plants provide a Mediterranean mood.

Cool schemes

Since few plants like to be disturbed by constantly moving water, most planting is done next to the water feature, although leaves and flowers will soften the edges. Shape of foliage and habit of growth are all-important, and you'll be surprised how many shades of green there are for colour contrasts. Including a few evergreens, such as hellebores, will ensure there is interest throughout the winter months.

◀ Asplenium scolopendrium *'Crispum'*.

▼ Helleborus orientalis.

WATER PLANTS

Ferns

Ferns make fronds of green, large or small, smooth or crimped, broad or narrow, beside the water. You may be able to grow smaller ferns in a crevice in a wall.

Adiantum capillus-veneris (maidenhair fern) – fine, wiry stems with delicate, shell-like leaves; good in shady waterside crevices
ht and sp 15–30cm/6–12in
Asplenium scolopendrium (spleenwort or hart's tongue fern) – tapering, slightly leathery, wavy-edged fronds of bright apple-green (evergreen)
ht and sp 60cm/2ft
A.s. 'Crispum' – densely growing, upright, very frilled, apple-green fronds (evergreen)
ht and sp 60cm/2ft
A.s. Marginatum Group – (various upright and frilly-edged hart's tongue ferns, some with tooth-edged fronds)
ht 35cm/14in
sp 45cm/18in
Dryopteris affinis (golden-scaled male fern) – tall stalks have golden brown scales and the unfurling fronds are yellowish green, turning deep green (often evergreen)
ht and sp to 80cm/32in
D. erythrosora – smaller, deciduous variety with reddish colouring
ht 60cm/2ft
sp 38cm/15in
D. filix-mas (male fern) – very tall, clump-forming variety with mid-green foliage
ht and sp to 1.2m/4ft
Phegopteris connectilis (beech fern) – low-growing, pale-green, bracken-like fern in light yellowish green, for acid soils
ht 20–25cm/8–10in
sp 30cm/12in
Polystichum setiferum (soft shield fern) – soft, waving fronds of mid-green for dappled shade (evergreen)
ht 60cm–1.2m/2–4ft
sp 45–90cm/18–36in
Woodsia polystichoides (holly fern) – small, pale green fern, native of rocky places and ideal for moist, but constantly draining, areas such as in a wall by a

▲ Hosta *'Tokudama'*.

spout (needs shelter/protection from frost)
ht and sp 20cm/8in

Water lilies for a tiny pond

Water lilies (*Nymphaea* cultivars) thrive in still water and a sunny spot. Several are small enough for a miniature pond in a barrel.
N. tetragona 'Helvola' – clear yellow, star-shaped flowers; tiny, maroon-mottled leaves
N. 'Pygmaea Rubra' – rose-pink flowers, deepening to blood red; copper-green leaves
N. 'Sulphurea' – bright yellow flowers raised well above the surface; brown-marked leaves
N. 'Daubeny' – starry blue, yellow-stamened, scented flowers; pointed, olive-green leaves (needs min. 21°C/70°F water temperature summer and 10°C/50°F winter)

Other plants at home beside the water

Arum lily (*Zantedeschia aethiopica*) – white spathes on erect, fleshy stems and broad, smooth, tapering leaves
ht 45–90cm/18–36in
sp to 60cm/2ft
Astilbe (*Astilbe*) – feathery plumes of flowers in red, cream and pink; good varieties include *Astilbe* 'Bridal Veil' (syn. 'Brautschleier') (creamy white), 'Fanal' (deep crimson), 'Sprite' (shell pink)

and *A. chinensis* var. *pumila* (dwarf, reddish pink), ht and sp 20–90cm/8–36in
Bleeding heart (*Dicentra spectabilis*) – hanging lockets of pink or white, feathery foliage
Candelabra primroses (*Primula* species) – erect stems of tapering or drumhead flowerheads; good varieties include *P. japonica*, *P. pulverulenta*, *P. secundiflora*, *P. vialii*
ht to 45–90cm/18–36in
sp 45–60cm/18–24in
Hellebores (*Helleborus* x *ballardiae* 'December Dawn', and varieties of *H. niger* and *H. orientalis*) – nodding, cup-shaped flowers in plum or white, some pink-stained or with pretty markings
ht and sp to 30cm/12in
Meadowsweet (*Filipendula*) – fuzzy, deeply scented flowers in creamy white, red and pink; good varieties include *F. rubra* (red stems, peach pink flowers), *F.r.* 'Venusta' (rose pink flowers – both these can be very tall), *F. ulmaria* (creamy white – smaller)
ht 60cm–1m/2ft–3ft or more
Hostas (*Hosta* cultivars) – shade-loving plants with broad, attractive leaves and heads of tubular, bell-shaped flowers (see page 69)

tranquil gardens

Tranquillity is one of the most desirable qualities in a garden and many gardeners seek to create areas of rest and contentment that will help them to survive the rigours and continual demands of modern-day living. Garden ponds, as described in the previous section, are part of this soothing process, as well as fragrant plants and cool and shaded areas. The simplicity of Zen gardens helps in the quest for spiritual enlightenment and an understanding of the purpose of life.

designing a meadow garden

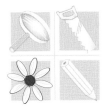

A wildflower meadow humming with insect activity in high summer is a rare and delightful sight. Even in a small garden you can create a mini-meadow, either by leaving an area of lawn to grow and produce its own colony of plants or by the deliberate introduction of a mix of wild flowers and grasses suited to the soil type.

▲ *Transforming an area of this large garden into a meadow will attract wildlife whose survival depends on nectar-rich plants.*

GARDEN DATA

location:	▦ Scotland
climate:	▦ cold/windy
soil type:	▦ thin and chalky
direction:	▦ west facing
aspect:	▦ sloping towards trees

Design brief

The open space designated for this small patch of meadow planting is part of a large garden which is planted very informally. The soil is thin and chalky – ideal conditions for a dry-meadow planting. The owners want to add a splash of summer colour which will be visible from the house and are prepared to learn how to use a scythe in order to 'mow' the meadow in late summer. Otherwise, apart from the removal of unwanted weeds, it will be left untouched.

Design solution

To avoid unwanted competition from vigorous grasses we stripped the existing turf. We undertook no further soil preparation other than removing surface stones. There are many possibilities for flower and grass mixtures and even for a mini-cornfield. Here we chose a selection of plants which can cope with dry conditions and the slightly alkaline soil. Apart from *Myosotis*

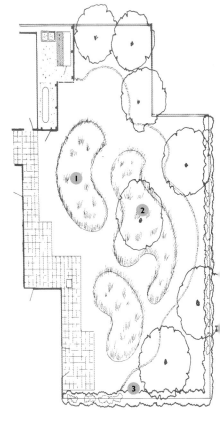

– 25 m x 13 m / 80 ft x 42 ft –

(forget-me-not) the plants are summer-flowering and after two or three years will establish and start to spread more or less vigorously.

flowering cherry

◀ *A flowering cherry is a focal point in the centre of our designer's garden.*

ox-eye daisy

▶ *A traditional country hedge is a wonderful boundary for a meadow garden.*

traditional hedge

◀*Ox-eye daisies were once common in meadows and will grow well in a garden.*

plants for a meadow garden

The key to a successful meadow garden is to encourage nature to do its best, not try to interfere with it. Having prepared the ground thoroughly, start your meadow by sowing seed in spring. Nature does the rest. Some plants will thrive in a wide range of meadow conditions, but patience is critical to success.

Before you sow

Perennial weeds can be a problem in a meadow garden and eliminating as many as possible before you begin is the aim. Start with a bare plot. Some meadow growers advocate ploughing. In a smaller area you might consider rotovating, laying down black plastic for a year to suppress weeds, or even spraying the whole area with a harmless weedkiller (a glyphosate type).

Planting with potatoes for a year (a well-known clearing crop) is also a recommended way of preparing the ground. Those devoted to the task will remove perennial weeds by hand before they begin. Most meadows thrive on soil that is not too fertile so it may be best to remove the top layer of earth in an established garden, especially if the soil is of the fertile, loamy type or has been well cultivated over the years.

To select plants that will be at home in the type of soil and situation you have to offer, spend some time assessing this first, and then browse over the catalogues. The three main types of soil are the more fertile, medium to heavy soils (sometimes called 'loamy' or 'pasture'), and the poorer chalk and sandy soils. You also need to assess whether the soil is dry/well-drained (usually in a sunny, open position) or whether it tends to be moist (and often more shaded).

◀ Briza media *is a perennial grass.*

ADAPTABLE MEADOW PLANTS

The following will thrive in many meadow situations. We give common names in these lists, as seed is sold under these names.

aquilegia	knapweed
bird's foot trefoil	lady's bedstraw
black medick	meadow clary
common daisy	meadow cranesbill
cow parsley	ox-eye daisy
cowslip	primrose
dandelion	ragged robin
forget-me-not	scabious
goat's beard	self-heal
kidney vetch	white campion
drumstick allium	yarrow

▲ Allium sphaerocephalon, *commonly called drumstick allium.*

▲ *Meadow clary attracts bees and insects.*

Ready-mixed seed such as 'cornfield mix', 'hay meadow mix' (early-flowering), 'flowering lawn mix' (for shorter grass), and 'meadow flowers' (the most wide-ranging) are available. You will also find mixtures on offer for the various soil types, including acid or alkaline soils. Be prepared to spend some time selecting plants that will be at home in your plot. Otherwise of course, you can chance your luck and learn as you go.

Meadow grass

It's important to have suitable grass so that it doesn't dominate the wild flowers but instead acts as a foil for them. The grass itself will produce plumes of beige and buff flowerheads

MEADOW PLANTING

Meadow in a lawn

You can sow meadow seeds directly onto grass in spring or autumn. Cut the grass as low as possible and rake the lawn well to open it up. Broadcast a general 'meadow mixture' seed and rake in lightly. (The soil should be moist.) Firm the area with a roller.

Keep the grass fairly closely cut during the first year so that it does not get ahead of the flowers. From year two, cut the grass in early May, then after summer flowering in late August, and again in late October.

Moist meadow plants

astilbe	celandine
lady's smock	meadowsweet
meadow buttercup	mimulus
trollius	purple loosestrife

Plants for chalk and limestone

comfrey	cowslip
flax	harebell
hawkbit	knapweed
pinks, Cheddar	toadflax

Shady meadow plants

These plants are also suitable for growing under trees.

betony	bugle
forget-me-not	foxglove
herb robert	purple loosestrife

Bulbs, corms and tubers for naturalizing

Scatter the bulbs and plant where they land, using a bulb planter. Plant each bulb with twice the amount of soil above it as its own depth. Bulbs are hungrier than true meadow plants and can benefit from an annual dressing of a high-potash fertilizer.

Plants marked (W) are also suitable for woodland conditions and shade.

bluebell (W)
crocus
celandine
daffodil (*Narcissus pseudonarcissus*)
grape hyacinth
lily-of-the-valley (W)
snowdrop (W)
wild garlic (*Allium ursinum*) (W)
wood anemone (W)
wood tulip (*Tulipa sylvestris*) (W)

Plants for thin, dry soils

Also for windswept areas and coastal conditions. Plants marked (S) are for sandy soil.

California poppy (S)

clover	convolvulus
corncockle (S)	corn marigold (S)
evening primrose (S)	flax
harebell	lupin
mullein	pinks, Cheddar
St John's wort	toadflax
vetch	yarrow

which are part of the charm of a meadow garden.

Grass seeds are also available for starting meadows, while some flower mixtures contain a suitable grass seed as well, so check when you buy. If in doubt ask your seed supplier for advice before buying.

Profile plants

Geranium pratense (meadow cranesbill) is one of the few meadow plants that requires rich soil. *Leucanthemum vulgare* (ox-eye daisy) thrives in a multitude of situations. *Briza media* (quaking grass) is a delightful grass for a meadow.

designing a cool, shaded garden

A shady site can be turned into a lush and leafy green oasis, or a woodland garden. It need not be without colour at most times of the year and can always be planted with a variety of leaf textures and shapes. Dry shade under the canopy of large trees is more difficult, but even here ivy or gaultheria will cope adequately.

Design brief

The north-facing garden forms a long rectangle, shaded on three sides by neighbouring trees and on the fourth side by the house. Some year-round interest is required together with planting to balance the tall surrounding trees. There is a small summer house at the far end.

Design solution

We decided to turn the shadiness of the site into a positive feature by creating an informal woodland area round the summer house. We planted graceful birches, which will still allow some light through to the woodland floor. We massed different ground-cover plants beneath the trees to flower at different times of the year. A camellia puts on a stunning spring show against the dark green backdrop of the surrounding yew hedge. The planting was surrounded by a deep bark mulch – leaf mould would be even better – and we marked a gently meandering path

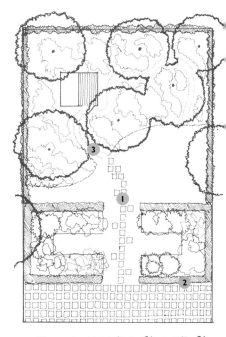

– 19 m x 11 m/60 ft x 35 ft –

with a coarser grade of bark chippings in a lighter colour. Nearer the house we contrasted the informality of the woodland with a geometric matrix of slabs set in closely mown grass. Formal box hedges enclose perennials and flowering shrubs and frame the path through the garden to the wood.

▲ *In this garden we decided to screen the summer house with trees to create an element of surprise and provide privacy.*

GARDEN DATA

location:	Kent
climate:	temperate
soil type:	neutral – alkaline
direction:	north facing
aspect:	overlooks railway bank

box hedge ②

▲ Flower beds are edged with clipped box.

bark chips ③

▲ Bark chippings are used as a path to the summer house, and to provide ground cover.

paving slabs ①

▲ Paving slabs are set in the mown lawn.

67

plants for a cool, shaded garden

The garden we designed has shade of its own and needed a selection of plants that would thrive in and enhance it. In other gardens you may wish to grow plants in a light position in order to create shade. Deciduous plants will ensure that shade is reduced to a pattern of shadows in winter when you want more light.

Green arbours

Climbing plants grown over an arbour or pergola can create areas of shade in a sunny garden. These structures need to be strongly made – or, if you buy them in kit form, well assembled and installed – as they eventually bear a strong weight and it's disheartening to have to dismantle and rebuild them just as the plants are reaching their peak of glory. Ideally a pergola should lead somewhere or extend all the way along the length of a wall. Plants to grow up trees or large shrubs should be planted some distance from the roots and guided towards their host with canes or strings.

Plants for creating shade

Honeysuckle (*Lonicera periclymenum*) and wisteria (*Wisteria sinensis*) are two lovely scented climbers, along with a few climbing roses. Russian vine (*Fallopia aubertii,* syn. *Polygonum aubertii*) is a terrifically fast climber for creating green shade, though it will need to be kept severely within bounds – not for nothing is it known as mile-a-minute vine. A true vine, *Vitis coignetiae* provides cooling green leaves that overlap to form a lovely density, followed by a warm red glow in autumn. The hop plant (*Humulus lupulus*) is another leafy climber with flat, overlapping leaves, in green or a sharp greeny yellow, (*H. l.* 'Aureus'). All these are deciduous, but shade is not such an objective in the winter, when the twining stems create their own beauty and the extra light will be welcome.

Wall plants in shade

As climbers to provide all-year green in shady places the ivies (*Hedera helix*) are invaluable. Or for a sheltered, shady wall there is *Trachelospermum asiaticum*, with waxy, scented flowers. The climbing hydrangea, *Hydrangea petiolaris*, is a vigorous and tolerant wall plant which though deciduous looks good when bare.

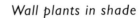
◄ *Astilbes are excellent shade plants.*

HOSTAS FOR SHADE

Hostas are the perfect plant for moist and shady places, with their generous mounds of overlapping, heart-shaped leaves and stems of small tubular flowers. They love the humus-rich soft earth under deciduous trees, where they get dappled shade. There is now a multitude of hostas, grown mainly for their leaves – often crinkled or rippled and having contrasting margins – in shades of green, golden-green or blue-green. Perhaps the best way to make a selection is to choose what appeals from your local plant centre. Some special cultivars are listed here. It's essential to protect hostas from slugs and snails, which are particularly partial to this snack.

Hosta selection
H. 'Blue Wedgwood'
Hosta fortunei var. *aureomarginata*
  (syn. H. 'Aureomarginata')
H. 'Frances Williams'
H. 'Halcyon'
H. 'Honeybells'
H. 'Sum and Substance'
Hosta sieboldiana var. *elegans*
H. *tokudama*
H. *undulata* var. *albomarginata*
H. *venusta*
H. 'Wide Brim'

▲ *The black birch has beautiful peeling bark.*

Profile plants

Betula nigra 'Heritage'
BLACK BIRCH

This is a tall but graceful birch for a woodland area, its whitish young bark peels to reveal orange-brown new bark. In early spring it bears long brown catkins and the brown leaves turn yellow in autumn.

ht 18m/60ft
sp to 12m/40ft
Soil and situation
Fertile, moist soil; shade.

Ajuga reptans
BUGLE

A low-growing, spreading woodland plant with whorls of small, deep blue or bronze flowers in spikes above the small green leaves.

ht 15cm/6in
sp 60cm/2ft
Soil and situation
Moist soil and partial shade.

Astilbe 'Fanal'
ASTILBE

There are many different astilbes for growing in moist conditions, mainly in cream or shades of pink. 'Fanal' is an unusual variety in deep red with very dark foliage.

ht 60cm/2ft
sp 45cm/18in

▶ Ajuga reptans *has spikes of deep blue flowers.*

Soil and situation
Dry soil and semi-shade.

designing a fragrant garden

A scented garden is essentially a romantic and feminine garden and is at its best on a warm summer's evening. The best site, even if it is just one corner of a larger plot, is a sheltered, warm position. Most fragrant plants release their perfumes in warm air and you will enjoy their scent more if it is not being blown clean away.

▲ The narrowness of this garden will be disguised by the clever use of screens that also provide shelter from the wind.

GARDEN DATA

location:	▪▪ Cornwall
climate:	▪▪ variable – mild
soil type:	▪▪ slightly acid
direction:	▪▪ south facing
aspect:	▪▪ rural valley

The design solution

This garden is long and narrow and the restricted feeling of a corridor is made worse by the long straight path which splits the garden into two even narrower slivers.

We designed a more sensuous, but simple, ground pattern, employing wide, curving borders with a slim ribbon of grass running between them and screens to shelter each garden room. These both help contain the perfumes of the plants and act as supports for some of the climbing plants. There is a bench from which colour, form and scent can be enjoyed, and the garden is lit on summer evenings to encourage you to linger on with your glass of Chardonnay. We used romantic whites, creams, soft yellows and blues in this scheme.

The grass path provides a lush, green carpet through the garden that does not distract from the scented air and the hum of bees.

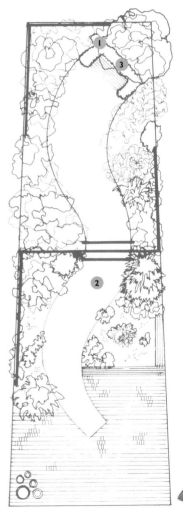

– 15 m x 6.5 m/48 ft x 21 ft –

screens

▶ *Willow fences
provide shelter.*

lawn

*he lawn curves intriguingly,
g a sense of discovery.*

seat

▲ *A seat surrounded by scented plants
offers an ideal place to unwind.*

plants for a fragrant garden

Plants in the scented garden are carefully arranged to ensure that there is something to offer at almost any time of year and at every level of the garden. There are both fragrant and aromatic plants, including those which flower at nose level and those whose perfume rises up from the ground.

Profile plants

Philadelphus 'Belle Etoile'
MOCK ORANGE

A heavenly scent of orange blossom drifts from the creamy white, four-petalled flowers in early summer. In this species the flowers have a dash of maroon at the centre, and the shrub is small enough for any garden. Should be pruned after flowering.

ht and sp 2m/6.5ft

Soil and situation

Well-drained soil; sun or partial shade.

Erysimum × allionii
(syn. *Cheiranthus × allionii*)
SIBERIAN WALLFLOWER

This is a wallflower with stunning bright orange colouring and a powerful scent to match. A short-lived perennial, it is always grown as a spring and early summer bedding plant.

ht 40cm/16in

sp 30cm/12in

Soil and situation

Fertile, well-drained soil, preferably neutral or alkaline, and a position in full sun.

Viola odorata
ENGLISH VIOLET
OR SWEET VIOLET

A spreading and very fragrant violet, flowering all spring with deep violet purple flowers, sometimes white or pink. Violets are lovely low-growing plants for naturalizing in moist, cool places. Various named hybrids are grown (known as florists' violets), including the double violet 'Duchesse de Parme' and the pink-flowered 'Coeur d'Alsace'.

ht 15cm/6in

sp to 40cm/16in

Soil and situation

Fertile, well-drained soil in a semi-shaded position, or in sun as long as the ground is cool.

▶ Erysimum x allionii, *Siberian wallflower.*

◀ Philaidelphus *'Belle Etoile' or mock orange.*

Shrubs and trees for scent

Choisya ternata
(Mexican orange blossom)
(see pages 40–41)
Daphne mezereum – small, heavily
scented, purple-pink flowers in
winter/spring; must have alkaline soil
ht to 90cm/3ft

Caution: the berries are poisonous

Fothergilla major and *F. gardenii* –
scented, cream-coloured flowers
in spring
Magnolia grandiflora – magnificent tree
for sheltered areas; summer flowers
with a spicy fragrance
ht 9m/30ft
See also *Magnolia stellata*
(Star magnolia)
(see page 21)
Rhododendron luteum
(Ghent azaleas) – rhododendrons and
azaleas are not noted for fragrance,
but these hybrids have a strong, warm
honeysuckle scent and brilliant
yellow flowers in late spring; need
acid soil
ht to 3m/10ft
Sambucus (Garden elder) – upright,
cone-shaped panicles of tiny, scented,
cream-coloured flowers in early
summer
Syringa cultivars (lilacs) – flowers in
purples through to white, with wafts
of the most heady scent towards the
end of spring *ht 1.8–4.5m/6–15ft*
Viburnum cultivars – all the winter-
and spring-flowering viburnums have
delicious scent

A SELECTION OF SCENTED PLANTS

Scent in full summer

Heliotropium arborescens (syn. *H. peruvianum*)
heliotrope or cherry pie plant
Lathyrus odoratus sweet pea
Lavandula species lavender
Lilium regale and other lilies
Matthiola bicornis night-scented stock
Matthiola incana Brompton stock
Nicotiana tobacco plant
Pelargonium crispum and *P. x fragrans*
pelargoniums with scented leaves
Petunia hybrids petunias
Phlox paniculata garden phlox

▲ *Midsummer flowering* Lilium regale.

Scent in spring and early summer

Convallaria majalis lily-of-the-valley
Dianthus species pinks and carnations
Erysimum species (syn. *Cheiranthus*) wallflowers
Hesperis matronalis dame's violet or sweet
rocket
Hyacinthus cultivars hyacinth
Narcissus jonquilla (jonquil) and many other
narcissi
Paeonia 'Sarah Bernhardt' – peony in apple
blossom-pink
Primula vulgaris and *P. auricula* primrose and
auricula

Roses for perfume

Almost all roses are perfumed but this is a
selection of favourites
Rosa 'Boule de Neige' – a repeat-flowering
bourbon rose with large flowers like white
camellias
ht 1.5m/5ft
Rosa 'Cardinal Richelieu' – a gallica rose, with
dusky purple-red flowers
ht 1.5m/5ft
Rosa centifolia 'Robert le Diable' – a cabbage
rose, in mauve, pink, violet and crimson
ht 1.2m/4ft
Rosa damascena – the damask rose has
varieties in white, pink, red
ht to 1.5m/5ft

Rosa gallica officinalis – deep crimson/striped
(see page 13)
Rosa 'Margaret Merril' – small floribunda or
cluster-flowered rose with delicate flowers in
blush white
ht 75cm/30in
Rosa moschata (musk rose) – creamy-white
old-fashioned climber
ht to 4m/13ft
Rosa 'Mme Pierre Oger' – a bourbon rose,
globular flowers in silvery pink all summer
ht 1.5m/5ft
Rosa 'Penelope' – a hybrid musk with flowers
in pale salmon pink all summer
ht to 1.2m/4ft
Rosa rugosa 'Blanc Double de Coubert' –
rugosa rose with white flowers all summer; big
red hips
ht 1.8m/6ft
Rosa 'Zéphirine Drouhin' – climber for wall or
trellis with masses of deep rose-pink flowers
all summer (suits a shady wall)
ht 3.6m/12ft
Rosa 'William Lobb' – a repeat-flowering old
moss rose with deep crimson flowers fading
to pale violet
ht 1.8m/6ft

designing a Zen garden

Buddhist monks designed the earliest Zen gardens around 900 years ago. In these gardens austere, abstract arrangements of rocks, water and plants represent nature in miniature. Western gardeners have returned again and again to this deceptively simple combination of materials to try to recreate this timeless style.

▲ *Recent travels in the Far East inspired the owner of this rectangular plot to design a minimalist Japanese garden.*

The brief

Steve travelled extensively in the Far East before recently acquiring his first house. His rectangular garden is ideally shaped and he would like to use this to advantage to create a minimalist garden with a Japanese influence.

The design solution

For complete privacy and shelter we enclosed the garden on three sides, using screening trellis panels wired to thick bamboo poles. This focuses attention entirely on the garden, ignoring the surrounding landscape and buildings. The basic design flows through three distinct areas in the garden. Inside the boundary a hedge was planted, which will be clipped to form hill shapes as it grows. Large rocks, smaller boulders, pebbles and paddle stones were carefully chosen to complement each other in size, markings and colour, positioned to create a balanced, asymmetric design. The main surface material is fine stone chippings, raked to suggest the flow of water. Stepping stones lead to a still, calm pool, positioned to reflect the ever-changing sky.

GARDEN DATA

location:	North West
climate:	temperate
soil type:	sandy
direction:	west facing
aspect:	urban

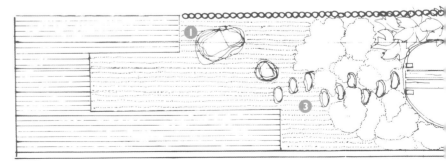

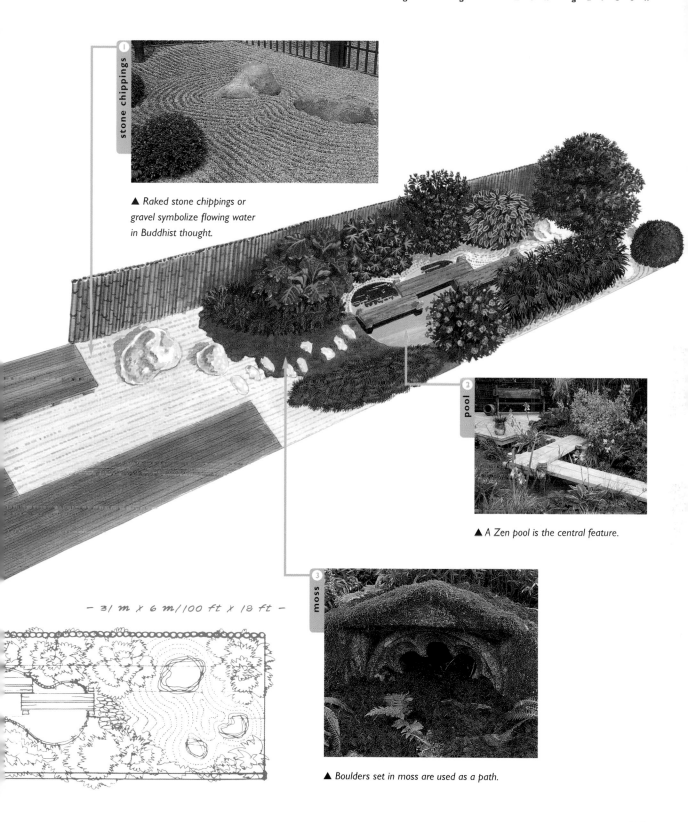

stone chippings

▲ Raked stone chippings or gravel symbolize flowing water in Buddhist thought.

pool

▲ A Zen pool is the central feature.

moss

– 31 m × 6 m/100 ft × 18 ft –

▲ Boulders set in moss are used as a path.

75

plants for a Zen garden

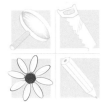

Restraint is the theme in planting a Zen garden. Green is the main colour from plants, to contrast with the natural materials used in the garden. A limited amount of blossom – ideally in red – is permitted. The best plants are bamboos; evergreen, glossy-leaved shrubs; and Japanese maples or a flowering cherry tree.

Bamboos and their care

Closely related to grasses and sedges, bamboos are evergreen, and as well as providing architectural shapes and delightful foliage, they also bring gentle movement and rustling sound to the garden. They grow up to 4m/13ft, in some species even more, and can make island clumps whose spread may sometimes overstep the limits (but see below) as well as lovely hedging and screening plants. Their hollow, woody culms take about three years to mature into canes. The canes are high in silica, which makes them very strong, and they can be cut for use, either as plant supports or for more ambitious projects such as screening. Bamboos are not all fully hardy and are best grown in a sheltered place.

Cultivation

Bamboos appreciate moisture, so when you plant them add plenty of fibrous organic material such as coir or – if you can get hold of it – chopped straw, to absorb and retain water. Don't use garden compost, however, as it will be too rich. An occasional feeding with calcium silicate will help them to grow strong culms but otherwise they need no supplementary feeding.

The best time for planting out bamboos is in spring, and it should be just before it rains. The leaves should not be allowed to become dry as they will quickly wither and die,

◀ *Japanese maples suit a Zen garden.*

so look after them until the plants are established by spraying them with water. You can restrict the spread of bamboo by digging around the clump at the desired limits and inserting a rigid, non-perishable plastic collar about 30cm/12in deep or to the depth of the roots.

Profile plants

Acer palmatum var. *heptalobum* 'Rubrum'
JAPANESE MAPLE

More of a shrub than a tree, this form of the Japanese maple has bronze leaves which are red as they first open and turn a fiery red in autumn. Its spreading and contorted branches give a very authentic Zen appearance

ht and sp to 6m/20ft
Soil and situation
Fertile, moist but well-drained soil,

◄ *Bamboos are essential in any Zen garden.*

preferably neutral or acid, and a sheltered position.

Camellia japonica
CAMELLIA

There are literally thousands of Japanese camellias, a most magnificent group of evergreen shrubs with dark green, polished leaves and luscious peony-like winter flowers (also other forms, including single, semi-double and double). The flowers must have shelter from morning sun in areas prone to frost as hastily melted frost makes the petals brown. *C. j.* 'Alexander Hunter' is semi-double, deep red, with yellow stamens; 'Paul's Apollo' (aka 'Apollo') has red, semi-double flowers and suits the British climate. 'Dr. H. G. Mealing' is blood red and semi-double; 'Kouron-jura' is dark red and fully double; 'Letitia Schrader' has dark red, large peony flowers.

ht to 8.5m/26ft
sp 7.3m/24ft

◄ *A red form of* Camellia japonica.

Soil and situation
Must have moist, fertile, well-drained, acid soil and should be mulched with shredded bark. In the northern hemisphere a sheltered north- or west-facing position is ideal.

HARDY BAMBOOS FOR SMALL GARDENS

Chusquea culeou (Chilean bamboo) – delicate, whitish green-leaves
ht 4.5m/15ft
Fargesia murieliae (umbrella bamboo) – greyish-green culms and apple-green leaves
ht 3.6m/12ft
Phyllostachys nigra var. *henonis* green – very leafy, not completely hardy
ht 9m/30ft
Phyllostachys viridiglaucescens – green and very leafy, not completely hardy
ht to 7.5m/25ft
Pleioblastus auricomus – yellow and green variegated leaves; purple-green culms
ht 1.5m/5ft
Pleioblastus simonii 'Variegatus' (syn. *Arundinaria simonii* 'Variegata') – white-striped leaves
ht to 3m/10ft
Pleioblastus variegatus – cream-striped leaves and pale green culms
ht 75cm/30in
Pseudosana japonica (arrow bamboo) – olive- green culms mature to light beige
ht to 4.5m/15ft
Sasa veitchii – white-edged green leaves and purple culms
ht to 1.8m/6ft
Semiarundinaria fastuosa (Narihira bamboo) thick green culms mature to dark red
ht 6m/20ft
Yushania anceps (anceps bamboo) – shiny, dark green culms, arching when mature
ht 2–3m/6.5–10ft

container gardening

Containers steeped in colourful flowers and foliage are ideal for brightening patios and terraces. Additionally, they are superb for positioning at the sides of front doors and porches, where they instantly capture the attention of visitors. To ensure success, the compost needs to be watered several times each day when the weather is hot and dry. By using bedding plants and bulbs it is possible to change the display from one year to another.

plants for a large container

If your garden gets a good amount of sun then you can create the equivalent of a summer border in a large container. The only thing to watch out for is size but, with care, you can contrive many excellent effects with a variety of colours. Any number of plants can be grouped together.

▲ *Patio roses such as the white 'Bianco' carry a mass of small shapely flowers in summer. They repeat flower throughout the year.*

One idea would be to grow sweet peas, *Lathyrus odoratus*, up a trellis or wigwam of poles at the back of the container. Make sure that you can cut the flowers because regular snipping produces more buds. The fairly low-growing pink geranium, *G. macrorrhizum*, can be placed in the middle, backed by the silver-leaved lamb's tongue, *Stachys byzantina*, with some pinks, *Dianthus*, planted in the front. For this scheme use scented pinks, such as 'Mrs Sinkins', an old cottage-garden favourite, white with feathery petals and an unrivalled scent. 'Doris' and 'Little Jock' are two good modern pinks, both scented, pale pink on the outside with darker markings in the centre. If the container is large enough then you can plant two penstemons to add a darker shade of red and give the scheme more emphasis. The best choice would be *P.* 'Andenken an Friedrich Hahn', which used to be called 'Garnet', with deep red flowers through summer into autumn, unless winter arrives very early.

A varied container of pink, red and white miniature roses

One of the easiest containers to design is composed of small roses that are available in a number of colours – red, white and pink. Small roses come in three groups, patio roses that grow to 45–60cm/1½–2ft, dwarf polyantha roses that are about the same size, and miniature roses that are generally slightly smaller.

To design an effective display start by planting one of the smaller cluster-flowered bush or floribunda roses to act as a centrepiece. The bright red 'Evelyn Fison' would be a good choice but, if you want a quieter display, 'English Miss',

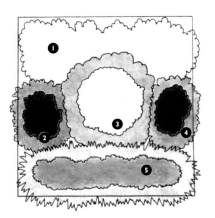

● Stachys byzantina
❷ Lathyrus odoratus
❸ Geranium macrorrhizum
❹ Penstemon 'Andenken an Friedrich Hahn'
❺ Dianthus

▲ *A good pink, red and white scheme for a container in summer. The pinks and sweet peas smell delicious, which adds to the attraction.*

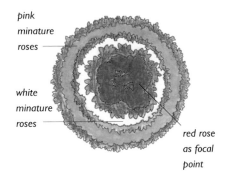

pink miniature roses

white miniature roses

red rose as focal point

▲ *Circular beds or containers planted with roses always catch the eye in summer. Include scented roses if possible, and feed them too.*

pink, or 'Margaret Merril', white with
pink buds, are both lovely roses and
exceptionally fragrant. All these
floribundas will grow to 75–90cm/
2½–3ft or slightly more. Then surround
the centre rose with red, pink or white
miniature roses. Both pink roses on the
inside surrounded by white on the
outside, and white surrounded by pink
look most attractive.

Since most patio roses have a spread
of 45cm/1½ft you need to allow this
distance between each plant. If you use
miniature roses you halve that distance.
'Bianco' and 'Greenall's Glory' are both
white patio roses, 'Pour Toi' is a white
miniature rose and 'Katharina Zeimet'
and 'Yvonne Rabier' are both attractive
dwarf white polyanthas. Suitable pink
roses include the patio roses 'Jean
Mermoz', 'Queen Mother' and 'Fairy
Changeling'; 'Dresden Doll' is a shell-
pink miniature moss rose, while 'Coral
Cluster' and 'Nathalie Nypels' are pink
dwarf polyanthas.

The ideal feed for roses is well-rotted
manure or compost but this may not be
possible if you are growing roses in a
container. Feed with bonemeal in the
autumn and then add a balanced fertilizer
in the spring. Roses should be pruned
hard in late winter or early spring to keep
them within bounds, and to encourage
new growth. Cut them back to a half or a
quarter of the original height, removing
any dead or damaged wood completely.

▶ *A wigwam planted with sweet peas and
nasturtiums makes an unusual focal point in a
small garden in summer.*

plants for foliage

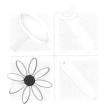

Very often container gardens are small and shady places where the sun seldom reaches. Such gardens are often unsuitable for colourful plants, and the answer is to use a variety of foliage plants. There are several attractive combinations that can create wonderful effects in containers.

The importance of background

The first thing to think about in a small shady garden is the background, and a background of ivy, *Hedera*, that remains green throughout the year is suitable and easy. Common ivy, *Hedera helix*, will grow almost anywhere and is still a good choice. However there are many varieties, both green and variegated, that are more interesting. Try *H. h.* 'Dragon Claw', which has a medium-sized soft green leaf, if you have a shady garden, or the variegated form *H. h.* 'Goldheart' with its gold-splashed leaves to give a touch of colour. Like all variegated ivies, this prefers some sun and shelter.

A container of ferns

Ferns are wonderful: soft, green, tolerant of deep shade, requiring little attention. A container of ferns is easy to plan and plant and if it is to be really successful it needs a story and focal point. The best fern to use for this is Wallich's wood fern, *Dryopteris wallichiana*. This is a striking plant. It is deciduous and carries erect strong, dark green fronds that are almost yellow when they first emerge in spring. The fronds are covered with dark brown or black scales. It can reach 1.8m/6ft in height although it is unlikely to grow quite so tall in a container. This can be surrounded by the evergreen Japanese holly fern, *Cyrtomium falcatum*, and the smaller evergreen hart's tongue fern, *Asplenium scolopendrium* – the variety 'Crispum' with its wavy mid-green fronds is more attractive than the species plant which is rather plain.

There are two choices to plant at the edge of the container. The small rusty-back fern, *Asplenium ceterach*, evergreen, with attractive fronds, only grows to 20cm/8in in height. This is a most useful plant for growing in walls or in cracks in paving. The other choice for a small fern is the common polypody, *Polypodium vulgare*, which reaches 30cm/12in and is also evergreen. This container gives

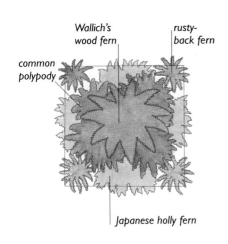

▲ *A container of ferns of different colours and leaf shapes can bring a cool shady garden to life in summer. There are a number to choose from.*

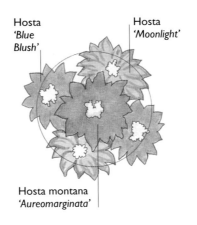

▲ *A container of hostas always looks attractive in a shady garden. Choose the varieties carefully to achieve the right balance of height and colour.*

◄ *A polypody fern is the centre of a green courtyard, including fatsia and a Japanese maple.*

▼ *Hostas grow well in containers as they prefer some shade and are less prone to slugs. Varieties of* H. undulata *have centrally marked leaves.*

differing heights, leaf shapes and colours throughout the year, and in the spring the grandest fern will rise up from the underworld and unfurl its leaves.

A container of hostas

Many gardeners will not attempt to grow hostas because they are loved by slugs and snails which cheerfully demolish plants wherever they are grown. They flourish much better in containers where the approach of the slug can be more readily repelled and, because they prefer shade to sun, they make an ideal choice for a shady patio garden. The beauty of hostas is the enormous variety of leaf colour, although they do carry spires of white to violet-blue flowers in summer. If you choose some of the smaller varieties, you can grow three or four hostas in a circular container 90cm/3ft in diameter. Good varieties to choose include: 'Moonlight' which reaches 50cm/20in in height, light green leaves that merge into yellow during the summer, with thin white margins around the edge; *H. montana* 'Aureomarginata', dark green leaves with splashed yellow margins; 'Blue Blush' and 'Hadspen Blue', both with a height and spread of 25cm/10in x 60cm/24in, blue-grey leaves, while those of 'Hadspen Blue' are larger; 'Blue Moon' is another, smaller, blue-grey hosta; and *H. fortunei* 'Albomarginata', a bit larger, has dull-green leaves with irregular cream-coloured margins.

plants for lasting interest

Evergreens should be present in every garden. They add interest, colour and shape, especially during the dull months of winter, and many, particularly conifers, change in colour in spring and summer. This provides varying colour tones to your garden at different times of the year.

Evergreen trees and shrubs for permanent containers

There are more evergreen trees suitable for growing in containers than might, at first, be apparent. The main container-grown small tree is the sweet bay tree, *Laurus nobilis*, found clipped into shape at the front of many town houses. These can be bought ready-shaped from nurseries, or they can be raised from semi-ripe cuttings taken in late summer. They grow fairly slowly and take time to develop.

Bay trees also have the added advantage that the leaves are of course useful for flavouring food.

Containers for camellias and rhododendrons

Another excellent small tree for the container garden is the camellia. There are many varieties and they need shade, moisture and acid compost to flourish, but they have unrivalled flowers in early spring, mainly in white, pink or red although there are a few yellow varieties, and some, such as 'Tricolor', have white, pink and red variegated petals.

The other tree or small shrub that shares similar requirements with camellias is the rhododendron, another excellent container plant. There are more varieties of rhododendron than any other garden plant, so you may find choosing difficult. They have a laxer habit than camellias,

◀ *A gravel forecourt can be used to arrange the plants symmetrically. The use of evergreens emphasizes the formal nature of the planting.*

▶ *The red berries of a standard holly tree brighten the autumn, complemented by the vivid Virginia creeper trained along the fence.*

and it is not so easy to underplant them with early spring bulbs. However, the flowers are lovely and come in many different shades and colours. Some are scented and there are many evergreen varieties that keep their interest when the flowering period is over.

Grow rhododendrons and camellias in suitably large individual containers, unless you have a large raised bed that has room for more than one. Suitable rhododendrons that are evergreen and do not usually reach more than 1.5m/5ft in height and spread include 'Azuma-kagami', pink; 'Berryrose', apricot-orange; 'Doc', rose-pink with deeper coloured margins and spots; 'Fabia', orange-red; 'Hatsugiri', crimson-purple; 'Hydon Dawn', pale pink to white; 'Kirin', deep pink; 'Moerheim', violet-blue; 'Mrs Furnival', light rose-pink; 'Percy Wiseman', peach-cream; 'Ptarmigan', white; 'Rose Bud', rose-pink; 'Scarlet Wonder', bright red; 'Seta', light pink; 'Snow Lady', semi-dwarf white; 'Songbird', violet-blue; 'Tessa Rosa', deep pink; and *R. russatum*, red to purple.

Holly trees

Holly trees may not seem an ideal choice for the container garden. Common English holly, *Ilex aquifolium*, and its varieties have prickly leaves (which are not ideal in a confined space). Both male and female plants are needed to produce berries. Most of the holly plants also have the problem of growing too large for their containers.

Nevertheless they are worth considering for growing in a larger formal garden, as they can be trimmed hard to make neat low-growing hedges and none of them grows very quickly. The varieties *I. a.* 'Argentea Marginata' and 'Silver Queen' have gold and white-edged leaves respectively that provide an added touch of colour. The other evergreen holly for the smaller garden is the Japanese holly, *I. crenata*, and its varieties.

GREY-LEAVED EVERGREENS

There are two other small trees that can be grown in containers, and both provide grey foliage throughout the winter. The first is the Australian cider gum tree, *Eucalyptus gunnii*. This is an excellent tree for a container because it can be treated as a shrub and cut back hard to the ground each spring. It will then throw up a number of young shoots throughout the summer with pale grey leaves that remain on the branches throughout the winter. The other small evergreen tree being grown more in containers, especially as the winters are generally rather milder, is the olive tree, *Olea europaea*. Olives are very slow growing and will not outgrow their situation too quickly, and eventually develop a rounded head with grey-green leaves with silvery grey undersides.

bedding plants

Bedding plants are the stand-by of the container garden. Many are annuals, some biennials, and others can be planted out as garden perennials once their flowering season is over. As their name implies, annuals grow, flower and die within one year. The majority are plants of the summer.

Bedding schemes for the winter and early spring

The stand-by bedding plants for all spring and winter containers are the coloured primulas, daisies and violas that have been bred to produce their brightly coloured flowers during the months of winter and early spring. They are best planted in separate containers rather than grouped together, as the varying habits and foliage do not mix very well. They are available in many colours.

Primulas

Winter and early spring-flowering primulas belong to the primula-polyanthus group. Those called polyanthus have longer flower stalks than primulas, and are grown as biennials. The seed is sown in the summer and the young plants come into flower in late winter and early spring the following year. Unless you are a real enthusiast, and want to raise your own plants from seed,

it is best to buy plants from the local nursery when they become available in winter and then plant them out.

Many primulas are very brightly coloured and the gardener can use them to experiment with schemes of primary colours, in red, yellow and blue, either planting the colours in sequence or in small blocks. As a general rule these bright colours look best if they are planted singly, one colour block succeeding another.

Daisies

When you look at the red, pink and white balls held aloft on 5cm/2in stalks rather like miniature dahlias, it is difficult to believe that the common daisy found on so many imperfect lawns is the ancestor of such highly developed plants. Those daisies sold as bedding plants have all been bred from the *Bellis perennis* of gardens, and the most common ones are from the Pomponette, Roggli and Tasso series. They are all reared as biennials, in the same way as the brightly coloured primulas, with the seed sown in the summer and the plants flowering early the following spring in full sun or partial shade.

As the colour range is limited a pleasant design can be created in any circular container with red plants in the centre, surrounded by rings of pink and then white flowers – or fill three similar

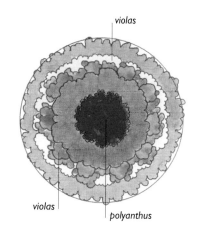

◄ Heathers, polyanthus, pansies and the red buttercup make a lovely arrangement in colours varying from deep red to pale pink.

▲ A blue and yellow winter/early spring bedding scheme that can be designed using winter pansies or varieties of polyanthus.

violas

violas

polyanthus

▶ The brilliant yellow-orange flowers of Primula forrestii surround the golden-yellow foliage of a small cypress tree.

small containers with a different colour in each and place them together.

Violas

Without any shadow of doubt, cultivated varieties (cultivars) of *Viola × wittrockiana* are the most valuable plants for any garden with containers, and they surpass all others for winter and early spring bedding schemes.

Many kinds of viola have been developed over the years, each with different characteristics, but they all flower for a long period and provide a real winter treat. Winter-flowering violas, bought and planted in mid-autumn, will still be flowering in spring and early summer the following year, over six or even nine months later.

As with primulas and daisies, violas are usually grown as biennials. They are either single-coloured or have the traditional pansy-type markings in two colours with a darker 'face' in the centre of the bloom. How they are planted must be a matter of personal choice, but groups of single-coloured varieties, either in separate containers or planted together in a large container, are extremely effective. This follows one of the first rules of gardening – plant in blocks of colour for the maximum impact. White flowers planted with those of a clear blue enliven the winter months, and this is a simple and most effective planting scheme.

It is best to confine violas to containers because in garden beds their bright colours only draw attention to the bare drab stalks of the other plants in winter.

◀ Petunias and marigolds go well together. Note the green foliage prevents this planting from becoming too garish.

There are so many summer annuals that a gardener might spend months each winter devising different plantings and colour schemes. Annuals are best used in three ways: as fringe plants to frame a border in summer, to fill any gaps, or to fill in a specific area and make a colour statement. The best example of the last is the park bedding schemes that can be seen in many towns and cities in the summer months.

In a container garden they can be used in all ways. If you have a large raised bed, then you can add white or red pelargoniums in summer. White is a good choice because it links all the other colours in the bed.

Red, white and blue

Individual containers can be used for individual plants and colour schemes, and the effect you achieve depends entirely on your choice of plants. Very often you can be too bold. The red, white and blue effect using violet-blue lobelias, the scarlet *Salvia splendens* and white geraniums can be a bit loud, especially in a confined space. Leave out the blue or red and the two colours work better together. There are a number of white and red annuals that you can plant, such as reddish-orange mimulus, red and pink busy Lizzie, *Impatiens*, red *Amaranthus caudatus*, red and white forms of *Begonia semperflorens* and white petunias.

Colour against a wall

Annuals are ideal for planting in wall pots. Here you should aim for a mass of mixed colours, mainly red and pink, but blue, purple, even orange, shades will not look out of place provided there are sufficient white plants to bind the scheme together. Geraniums, *Pelargoniums*, are a must. The trailing forms that hang down over the edge of the container are most useful for hiding a wall, and the scheme should include lobelias, busy Lizzies, many pelargoniums, schizanthus and fuchsias. This gives a bright glorious mixture.

If you prefer quieter colours, you can follow the same idea but concentrate on paler flowers. Mixed sweet pea, *Lathyrus odoratus*, can be grown in containers against a wall, and the wall pots above it can be filled with petunias from one of the softer mixed series, such as Milleflora Fantasy Mixed or Daddy Mixed. Even here a number of white plants, such as the petunia Supercascade White, will help the scheme to work, and some of the soft-coloured fuchsias can also be added.

SUMMER ANNUALS FOR A RIOT OF COLOUR

There was once a gardening programme on television that featured an elderly couple who planted out over 30,000 annuals around their caravan each year. In high summer they deadheaded and watered them twice every day. The effect was quite wonderful, and underlines both the possibilities of annuals and the importance of removing the dead flowers to encourage the plants to flower again and again. Once a flower has set seed, it thinks its job is done and stops flowering.

◀ *A brilliant display of annuals in high summer, planted to hide a wall. The containers are matched on either side to make a mirror display.*

❶ *Fuchsia* 'Gartenmeister Bonstedt'

❷ *Petunia* 'Lemon Plume'

❸ *Petunia* 'Carpet Mixed'

❹ *Schizanthus* 'Gay Pansies'

❺ Million Bells 'Terracotta'

❻ *Impatiens* 'Coral Bells'

❼ *Lobelia* 'Sapphire'

❽ *Tagetes* 'Safari Tangerine'

❾ *Pelargonium* 'Gillian'

Orange annuals for the autumn

Orange can be a difficult colour to blend with other plants but an individual container of orange, yellow and lemon marigold, *Tagetes* Marvel Mixed, planted with some nasturtium, *Tropaeolum*, gives a lift to autumn days. The leaves of the nasturtium will hang down over the container's edge, and the marigolds can stand in the centre.

You can substitute pot marigold, *Calendula officinalis*, for the African marigold, *Tagetes*, and achieve almost the same effect, although the flowers are smaller and less opulent. Add the leaves of both to late summer salads, and the petals of the pot marigold can be used for food colouring.

▶ *Nasturtiums, red geraniums and the red lily 'Fire King' make a brilliant red and orange corner on a patio in high summer.*

plants for an alpine garden

The small size of alpines makes them most suitable for growing in a container as they are neat attractive plants. Their only disadvantage is that so many flower in late spring and early summer, and if you want the bed to be colourful for the remainder of the year you have to choose with care.

Soil and site

The majority of alpines need a sunny open site, preferably facing south or south-west. If you want to create an alpine bed and cannot offer such a position in your garden, you can concentrate on those alpines that come from woodland areas and like moist soil and dappled shade. There are a number of these, and they are best grown in a peat substitute bed. Many gardeners make special raised beds for alpines, and this is most effective when the bed is constructed from natural stone, with cracks and crevices, in which many alpine plants flourish. If you are building a raised bed from bricks or stone and are using mortar to bind the material together, leave some gaps between the courses which can be filled with soil. Many alpines flourish in these situations.

It is essential that any growing medium should be free draining. The best compost to use is a mixture of two parts John Innes No. 3 or good quality loam topsoil (if available), mixed with one part of coarse grit and one part peat substitute. Add some slow-release fertilizer if you use topsoil. Make sure that there is a layer of hardcore in the bottom of the container, that there are plenty of drainage holes if you are planning to plant alpines in a trough or window box, and finally, when planted, cover the surface with a 1cm/½in layer of stone chippings. The chippings not only mulch the plants, retaining moisture during dry periods in the summer, but

▼ *Low stone troughs or old sinks are ideal containers for alpines. These must have free drainage. Check the requirements of the plants you choose: most alpines prefer a sunny open site.*

1. Aubrieta 'Greencourt Purple'
2. Saxifraga Moss Varieties Mixed
3. Fritillaria meleagris
4. Geranium dalmaticum
5. Gentiana aucalis
6. Armeria maritima
7. Pulsatilla rubra
8. Campanula carpatica 'Bressingham White'
9. Gypsophila repens 'Dorothy Teacher'

▲ To plant an alpine container garden, you should folllow the three steps shown here. First prepare a compost of two parts John Innes No. 3 to one part coarse grit and one part peat substitute. Space the plants out on the surface of your container where you want them.

▲ Firm all the plants in position, allow more room than you think between them, and then put as many decorative rocks on the container as you wish.

▲ Cover the surface of the container with a mulch of stone chippings. These help to retain the moisture in the compost and suppress weeds.

also help to smother weeds. Even though they are small do not plant alpines too close together as they spread quickly.

Some popular alpines

Aethionema (Stone cress) – evergreen or semi-evergreen sub-shrubs with clumps of pink flowers from late spring onwards. The most common are *A. armenum*, *A.*

grandiflorum and *A.* 'Warley Rose'. *Alyssum* and *Aurinia* – two closely related groups of clump-forming plants with evergreen leaves and yellow or white fragrant flowers. *Alyssum spinosum* has white flowers, *Aurinia saxatile* yellow. Rock jasmine, *Androsace* – these plants make dense cushions with single or clustered flowers. *A. lanuginosa* has soft pink flowers, *A. pyrenaica*, white flowers. *Arabis* (Rock cress) – mat- or cushion-forming plants suitable for growing in crevices. *A. caucasica* has white and pale pink flowers. *A. c.* 'Flore Pleno' has pure white double flowers.

Armeria maritima (Sea thrift) – cushion-forming plants whose pink flowers are familiar to everybody who visits the seaside. There are a number of species

and cultivars in deeper colours.

Aubrieta – this is the favourite plant for all cottage garden walls with evergreen grey-green leaves and violet and purple flowers that hang down in long tresses, covering the plant throughout the early summer months.

Campanula (Bellflower) – there are a number of small alpine bellflowers. They include: fairy's thimble, *C. cochleariifolia*, with white to lavender flowers; *C. carpatica*, white and blue flowers, spreads quickly; and Dalmatian bellflower, *C. portenschlagiana*, with deep purple flowers in late summer.

Celmisia (New Zealand daisy) – evergreen with white daisy-like heads with a pronounced yellow centre. *C. spectabilis* is particularly striking.

Cyclamen (Sowbread) – most attractive tuberous-rooted plants, generally with pink or white flowers. Varieties of *C. coum* flower in late winter and early spring. *C. hederifolium*, better known as *C. neapolitanum*, flowers in the autumn.

Erigeron karvinskianus (Fleabane or wall daisy) – small evergreen perennial, often grown down and in walls, with daisy-like flowers that open white and then turn through pink to red.

Erinus alpinus (Fairy foxglove) – a tufted perennial, evergreen in mild winters, that has a mass of white, pink or purple flowers. The plants usually self-seed.

Fritillaria – some of the small fritillaries look lovely in an alpine garden when they flower in late spring. The lovely snake's head fritillary, *F. meleagris*, only reaches 30cm/12in in height, while the yellow fritillary, *F. pontica*, is only half this size.

Gentiana (Gentians) – one of the most popular alpine plants, gentians are grown for their vivid blue, trumpet-shaped flowers. *G. alpina* and *G. aucalis* flower in late spring to early summer, and *G. sino-ornata* flowers in the autumn.

Geranium (Cranesbills) – only the smallest cranesbills qualify as suitable alpine plants. They include the evergreen *G. cinereum* with white or pale pink flowers, *G. c.* ssp. *subcaulescens* with vivid magenta flowers and black centres, and *G. dalmaticum*, usually evergreen, with bright pink flowers.

Gypsophila repens (Alpine gypsophila) – a spreading, mat-forming plant with white through to rose-pink flowers. The best variety is 'Dorothy Teacher', with its delicate pale pink flowers.

Helianthemum nummularium (Rock rose) – a dwarf evergreen shrub with bright yellow flowers in summer.

Linum (Flax) – *Linum arboreum* is a dwarf evergreen shrub with yellow flowers in late spring, and *L. suffruticosum* ssp. *salsoloides* is a cushion-forming perennial with white flowers, with pink or violet veins in summer.

Lithodora diffusa – small evergreen shrub with striking blue flowers in late spring.

Penstemon (Penstemons) – are better known as herbaceous perennials but there are some small mat-forming species that come from alpine regions. They include *P. newberryi* with deep pink flowers in early summer, and rock penstemon, *P. rupicola*, with pale flowers in late spring.

Phlox – there are many small alpine phloxes. They include moss phlox,

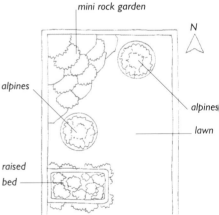

▲ *A complete area of the garden can be devoted to alpines in containers and this can be complemented by a mini rock garden in the sun.*

◀ *The saxifrage is a must for any alpine container gardener. These form springy mats of flowers in white, pink, purple and yellow.*

► *Alpines look at their best in a raised trough. The white clouds of Iberis sempervirens contrast with the deep pink of the sea thrift.*

P. subulata, with purple to white flowers in late spring, creeping phlox, *P. stolonifera*, with purple flowers in early summer, *P. adsurgens* with pink flowers and *P. douglasii* with mauve to crimson flowers.

Polygala calcarea (Milkwort) – mat-forming evergreen perennial with trailing stems of bright blue flowers in early summer.

Primula (Primrose) – ideal plants for a shaded alpine garden because they will not flourish in full sun. There are many coloured varieties available.

Pulsatilla (Pasque flowers) – popular clump-forming flowers whose foliage is among the finest in the alpine garden. The most popular are varieties of *P. vulgaris*, with purple flowers, *P. alba* has pure white flowers with deep yellow centres and *P. rubra* has red flowers.

Saponaria ocymoides (Rock soapwort, tumbling Ted) – the epitome of an alpine plant, tumbling Ted carries pale pink flowers from late spring through the summer. The variety 'Alba' is white.

Saxifraga (Saxifrage) – an important group for the alpine gardener. The majority form compact cushions with flowers ranging from white through to pink, purple and yellow. Among the most popular are *S. burseriana*, with white flowers, *S. exarata*, with yellow flowers throughout the summer and *S.* × *irvingii* 'Jenkinsiae', which is dark-centred with pale pink flowers in early spring.

Sedum (Stonecrop) – small sedums are good succulent plants for the alpine garden. Biting stonecrop, *S. acre*, has yellow flowers throughout the summer, *S. sieboldii* has coloured leaves and pink flowers, and the variety *S. s.* 'Mediovariegatum' has amazing yellow, blue and red leaves, and pink flowers.

Sempervivum (Houseleek) – large group of succulent plants notable for their extraordinary rosettes of leaves topped with pink flowers in summer. The most spectacular are cobweb houseleek, *S. arachnoides*, and common houseleek, *S. tectorum*, with red leaves.

Veronica prostrata (Prostrate speedwell) – mat-forming perennial with blue flowers and a number of good varieties.

▼ *A diagrammatic plan of an alpine garden with a colour scheme that could be achieved using several different plants from the list below.*

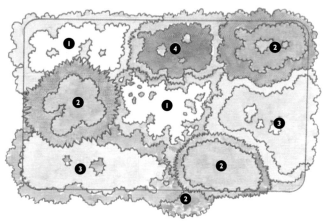

❶ White
Alyssum spinosum
Androsace pyrenaica
Campanula carpatica
 'Bressingham White'

❷ Pink
Aethionema '   ley Rose'
Geranium dalmaticum
Saponaria ocymoides

❸ Lavender/Purple
Aubrieta
Phlox stolonifera
Pulsatilla vulgaris

❹ Blue
Campanula
 cochleariifolia
Lithodora diffusa

index

PICTURE CREDITS
Liz Eddison, Designers: Bill Cartlidge, Tatton Park 2000 cov; Christopher Costin 29tr, 70bl, br; Paul Dyer 55b; Guy Farthing/Marshalls 49b; Folia Garden Designers 61b; Alan Gardner, Tatton Park 2000 cov; Marney Hall 37br; Susan Harman 73tr; Alan Sargent 57bl; Robin Templar Williams 60; Geoffrey Whiten 25bl, 77bl; Wynniatt-Husey Clark 83b; Wythall Gardening Club, Chelsea 2000 cov. Neil Holmes 28, 31tr, 47t, b, **57tr**. Harry Smith Collection 17tl, tc, 26br, 27, 30–31b, 35tr, 42l, 43t, 64l, r, 65, 70bl, 75tl, 78br.